REVISE EDEXCEL GCSE
Spanish

REVISION WORKBOOK

Series Consultant: Harry Smith

Authors: Jackie Lopez and Leanda Reeves

A note from the publisher

In order to ensure that this resource offers high-quality support for the associated Edexcel qualification, it has been through a review process by the awarding body to confirm that it fully covers the teaching and learning content of the specification or part of a specification at which it is aimed, and demonstrates an appropriate balance between the development of subject skills, knowledge and understanding, in addition to preparation for assessment.

While the publishers have made every attempt to ensure that advice on the qualification and its assessment is accurate, the official specification and associated assessment guidance materials are the only authoritative source of information and should always be referred to for definitive guidance.

Edexcel examiners have not contributed to any sections in this resource relevant to examination papers for which they have responsibility.

No material from an endorsed resource will be used verbatim in any assessment set by Edexcel.

Endorsement of a resource does not mean that the resource is required to achieve this Edexcel qualification, nor does it mean that it is the only suitable material available to support the qualification, and any resource lists produced by the awarding body shall include this and other appropriate resources.

Contents

Audio files

Audio files for the listening exercises in this book can be found at:
www.pearsonschools.co.uk/mflrevisionaudio

A small bit of small print

Edexcel publishes Sample Assessment Material and the Specification on its website. This is the official content and this book should be used in conjunction with it. The questions in this book have been written to help you practise what you have learned in your revision.
Remember: the real exam questions may not look like this.

Target grades

Target grades are quoted in this book for some of the questions. Students targeting this grade should be aiming to get some of the marks available. Students targeting a higher grade should be aiming to get all of the marks available.

Birthdays

 When are these people's birthdays?

F 1 Match the correct person to each birthday. Put a cross in the correct box below.

Gloria

Mi cumpleaños es el siete de junio.

Fran

Mi cumpleaños es el ocho de marzo.

Alejandro

Yo nací el catorce de junio.

María

Mi cumpleaños es el quince de julio.

Víctor

Celebro mi cumpleaños el once de diciembre.

	Víctor	Gloria	Alejandro	María	Fran
Example: 11th December	X				
(i) 14th June					
(ii) 8th March					
(iii) 15th July					
(iv) 7th June					

(Total for Question 1 = 4 marks)

 When are their birthdays?

 **Audio files**
Audio files can be found at:
www.pearsonschools.co.uk/mflrevisionaudio

G 2 Listen to these people talking about when their birthdays are. Put a cross in the correct box.

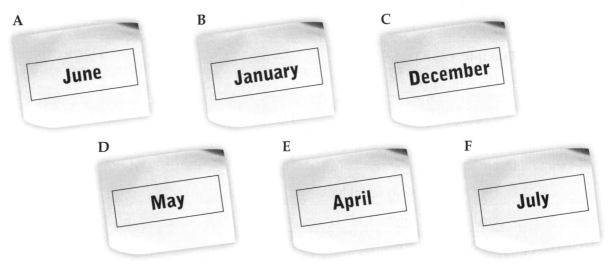

A June   B January   C December

D May   E April   F July

	A	B	C	D	E	F
Example:			X			
(i)						
(ii)						
(iii)						
(iv)						

(Total for Question 2 = 4 marks)

Physical description

My brother

C   **3**   Read Jorge's letter about his brother.

> ¡Hola amigo!
>
> ¿Quieres saber algo sobre mi hermano Raúl?
>
> Es mi único hermano. Es menor que yo pero parece más mayor. Es un chico guapo, pero muy, muy simpático. Dicen que se parece a mí, pero yo no lo creo. Raúl es muy alto, no es ni gordo ni delgado, pero está bastante cachas y le gusta ir al gimnasio. Lleva gafas y a veces se deja bigote. Admito que compartimos el mismo pelo rizado, largo y castaño, pero él lleva coleta y yo no. Yo suelo llevar el pelo suelto. Se parece más a mi madre que a mi padre.
>
> En tu próxima carta dime cómo es tu hermana mayor. ¿Te llevas bien con ella?
>
> ¡Hasta luego!
>
> Jorge

Put a cross in the **four** correct boxes.

Example: His name is Raúl.	X
A He is older than Jorge.	
B He is really tall.	
C He is ugly.	
D He looks strong.	
E He sometimes has facial hair.	
F He has Jorge's eyes.	
G He has Jorge's hair.	
H He looks more like their father.	

> Look out for words such as *pero* meaning 'but' as this may well affect the meaning of an earlier part of the sentence.

(Total for Question 3 = 4 marks)

Character description

 Teo's autobiography homework

 4 Part A

Read what Teo has written.

> Me llamo Teo Mateus Sidrón. Soy alto y fuerte y tengo el pelo oscuro y los ojos marrones.
>
> Soy muy trabajador en el cole y saco buenas notas. Me molan los deportes. Paso mucho tiempo jugando al baloncesto y soy miembro del equipo de vela. Tengo muchos planes para el futuro. ¡Hay tantas cosas que quiero hacer!

Put a cross against the **four** correct statements below.

Teo is:

Example: tall	X		
A short		**E** sporty	
B strong		**F** a loner	
C hardworking		**G** modest	
D lazy		**H** ambitious	

Part B

Teo goes on to talk about people. Read what he says.

> Con respecto a los amigos soy muy particular y exigente. Creo que hay que tratar a los demás con respeto, por lo tanto, no soporto a los que dicen cosas ofensivas. Para mí es muy importante que alguien me haga reír. También me gusta la gente que es inteligente. Sin embargo, no tengo tiempo para los que solo piensan en sí mismos.

What type of people does he talk about? Cross **four** boxes.

Example: gente respetuosa	X		
A gente extrovertida		**E** gente habladora	
B gente maleducada		**F** gente callada	
C gente graciosa		**G** gente inteligente	
D gente seria		**H** gente egoísta	

(Total for Question 4 = 8 marks)

Had a go ☐   Nearly there ☐   Nailed it! ☐

Countries and nationalities

 Julián's e-mail

5 Read this e-mail from a potential pen friend.

> ¡Hola!
>
> Me llamo Julián. Tengo catorce años y soy mitad inglés y mitad español. Dicen de mí que soy deportista y simpático. Vivo en el centro del pueblo con mis abuelos. Vivimos en un piso grande.
> ¿Qué me dices de ti?
> Saludos,
> Julián

What details are mentioned? Put a cross in the correct box.

Example: The boy is called ...

Javi	Raúl	Julián
		X

(i) He is ...

13 years old	14 years old	15 years old

(ii) He is ...

sporty	lazy	studious

(iii) He lives ...

in the countryside	by the coast	in a town

(iv) He lives with his ...

sister	brother	grandparents

(Total for Question 5 = 4 marks)

 My roots

6 Juan is talking about his family. What does he say about where they live and their nationality?

A	B	C	D	E	F
Juan	His father	His mother	His grandmother	The whole family	His aunt

Listen and complete the grid below with the correct letters.

Example: is Spanish	A
(i) lives in Spain.	
(ii) is German.	
(iii) is English.	
(iv) is American.	

(Total for Question 6 = 4 marks)

Brothers and sisters

My family

D

7   Read Ana's opinions about her family. What positive things does she say? Put a cross in the **four** correct boxes.

Example: Mi hermana menor es guapa.	X
A Paco es tonto.	
B María me hace reír, es divertida.	
C Me encanta mi hermano Carlos.	
D ¿Salir con mi hermana Susi? ¡No, gracias!	
E A mi hermano mayor le encanta el fútbol. ¡Qué aburrido!	
F Mi hermana mayor es simpática.	
G Juan es ruidoso.	
H Loli me ayuda con mis deberes, ¡es guay!	

> Sometimes you may not know the meaning of every word; however the rest of the sentence should give you a hint. In this instance, *divertida* will help you with the meaning of *reír*.

(Total for Question 7 = 4 marks)

My sister

C

8   Listen to Ursula talking about her sister, Marisol. Put a cross by the **four** correct statements below.

Example: Marisol is lots of fun.	X
A The sisters share a room.	
B Marisol is argumentative.	
C Marisol uses Ursula's things.	
D Marisol reads Ursula's diary.	
E Marisol listens to her sister's problems.	
F Marisol tells tales.	
G Marisol plays her music too loud.	
H Marisol helps her with her homework.	

(Total for Question 8 = 4 marks)

Family

 Family members

F 9 Read what these people say about their family.

Jorge
Tengo un hermano mayor.

Juan
Tengo un hermano gemelo.

Julieta
Mis padres están divorciados.

Milagros
Mi nieto se llama Kiko.

Montse
Me gusta mi madrastra.

Put a cross in the correct box.

	has divorced parents.	(i) has a grandson.	(ii) is a twin.	(iii) has a stepmother.	(iv) has an older brother.
Example: Julieta	X				
Jorge					
Milagros					
Juan					
Montse					

> If you don't know some vocabulary, do the ones you do know first and work out the others by a process of elimination.

(Total for Question 9 = 4 marks)

 My grandparents

B 10 Chico is talking about his grandparents. What makes them special?

Listen and put a cross in the **four** correct boxes.

Example: They live close by.	X
A They listen to his problems.	
B They help with his homework.	
C They buy him presents.	
D They talk to his parents.	
E They like the same activities.	
F They take him on holidays.	
G They are always positive.	

(Total for Question 10 = 4 marks)

Friends

 Marta's friends

D

11 Read what Marta has to say about her friends:

> Me llamo Marta y tengo tres amigos muy simpáticos. Antonio va al mismo colegio que yo. A menudo jugamos con el ordenador. Su madre es médico. Isabel es muy tranquila. Cuando tengo un problema, me ayuda. Su casa está cerca de la mía y a veces vamos juntas al cine. Su padre es profesor. Hugo es muy gracioso. Me hace reír. Su padre siempre le regala cosas. Por ejemplo, le compró un iPad para Navidad. Hugo tiene un grupo y a veces tocamos música juntos.

Put a cross in the correct box.

	Antonio	Isabel	Hugo
Example: Whose mother is a doctor?	X		
(i) Who in particular helps Marta?			
(ii) Who often receives presents?			
(iii) Who goes to the same school as Marta?			
(iv) Who is funny?			

(Total for Question 11 = 4 marks)

 My best friend

C

12 Loli is talking about her best friend, Javier. What is Javier like?

Write down the **four** correct letters.

Example:	H

A	sporty
B	funny
C	lazy
D	generous
E	small
F	clever
G	loud
H	popular
I	selfish

(Total for Question 12 = 4 marks)

Hobbies

At the leisure centre

F   **13** Read the information on the leisure centre display board.

A	B	C
Piscina olímpica	Equipos de fútbol	Canchas de tenis y bádminton

D	E	F
Clases de baile los miércoles	Club de informática	Clases de kárate cada martes

Match the hobbies of the people below to the activities offered at the lesuire centre. Put a cross in the correct box.

	A	B	C	D	E	F
Example: Martín loves martial arts.						X
1 Carlos likes raquet sports.						
2 María prefers dancing.						
3 Pablo loves water sports.						
4 Esther likes computers.						

(Total for Question 13 = 4 marks)

> If there are four marks available, make sure you put one tick against every name.

6   **An ideal weekend**

F   **14** Listen. Who wants to do what? Put a cross in the correct box.

	A I want to go to the library.	B I want to meet up with my friends.	C I want to go to the disco.	D I want to go swimming.	E I want to stay home.
Example: Juan			X		
1 Marta					
2 Luis					
3 Pablo					
4 Cristina					

(Total for Question 14 = 4 marks)

Sport

 Beach volleyball

B 15 Read this advert. Complete the sentences by putting a cross in the correct box.

Example: This activity is for people who want to have ...

A a rest.	
B fun.	X
C a holiday.	

Gran Fiesta Voleibol Playa

¿No sabes qué hacer estas vacaciones?
¿Quieres hacer ejercicio pero también buscas mucha diversión?
¡Pues esta fiesta es para ti!
Para jóvenes de entre doce y diecisiete años, este curso es ideal no sólo para mejorar tus habilidades deportivas – especialmente las de equipo – sino que también es una gran oportunidad para conocer a nuevos amigos.
Si te interesa ...
Ven el lunes día 3 a la cala de Mogán – zona verde.
Trae bañador, ropa deportiva y comida
(todos los refrescos están incluidos).
Precio: 15 euros el día.
Imprescindible autorización de padres o tutores.

(i) The festival is for ...

A all ages.	
B young children.	
C teenagers.	

(iii) You need to bring ...

A drinks.	
B appropriate clothing.	
C friends.	

(ii) One skill you might improve is ...

A speaking another language.	
B time management.	
C being a team player.	

(iv) Participation will not be possible without ...

A parental consent.	
B a sporting qualification.	
C pre-booking.	

(Total for Question 15 = 4 marks)

 Sport

G 16 Listen. Which sports do these young people mention?

 A    B    C    D    E    F

Put a cross in the correct box.

	A	B	C	D	E	F
Example:				X		
(i)						
(ii)						
(iii)						
(iv)						

(Total for Question 16 = 4 marks)

Arranging to go out

Saying no

17 Read this magazine article.

¿Sabes decir "NO"? ¿Eres bueno dando excusas?

Preguntamos a nuestros lectores qué excusas han usado para rechazar invitaciones no deseadas y aquí están los resultados de nuestra encuesta:

- La excusa más popular, con un veintitrés por ciento del voto, es la de tener que quedarse en casa para trabajar o estudiar.
- En segundo lugar está la excusa de que mis padres no me dejan. El veinte por ciento de los chicos entrevistados prefieren ésta.
- El siete por ciento suele decir que no puede salir porque tiene colegio o trabajo al día siguiente.
- El doce por ciento dice que tiene que cuidar a hermanos pequeños.
- Un dos por ciento dice que está esperando invitados en casa.
- El uno por ciento usa la excusa de estar malo.
- Para un diez por ciento, lo más fácil es decir que quieren ver algo guay como una peli en casa.
- A un valiente siete por ciento no le da vergüenza decir, simplemente, que no le apetece.
- ¡Y un uno por ciento de los entrevistados todavía usa la excusa de que tiene que lavarse el pelo!

Write the appropriate percentage for the **four** excuses in the grid below.

Excuse	%
Example: Have to study or work.	23
(i) Parents won't allow it.	
(ii) Feel ill.	
(iii) Don't feel like it.	
(iv) Have to look after younger brothers or sisters.	

(Total for Question 17 = 4 marks)

Going out

18 Conchi is talking to Juan. What do they agree about? What don't they agree about?

A the day	**C** the time	**E** the place to go	**G** the food
B the date	**D** the transport	**F** the meeting place	

Write the **four** correct letters in the table.

	✓ (agree)	✗ (don't agree)
Example:	E	
(i)		
(ii)		

(Total for Question 18 = 4 marks)

Last weekend

Last weekend

C

19 Read what these young people say about last weekend.

> **David:** Pasé unos días muy agradables. El sábado por la mañana fui de compras y después, antes de ir a la fiesta de mi primo Antonio, hice mis deberes. El domingo me quedé en la cama hasta el mediodía y después salí a cenar con mis amigos.
>
> **Luci:** Mi fin de semana no fue nada interesante. Mis padres nunca me permiten salir por la noche. ¡Es una pena! Me quedé en casa, leí, y me aburrí como siempre.
>
> **Javier:** Siempre hay algo que hacer los fines de semana. El viernes, por ejemplo, fui al polideportivo y el sábado di un paseo por el campo. Por desgracia, el domingo tuve que ordenar mi habitación.

Put a cross in the correct box.

	David	Luci	Javier
Example: Who stayed home all weekend?		X	
(i) Who did housework?			
(ii) Who went to a restaurant?			
(iii) Who read a book?			
(iv) Who spent time with their relatives?			

(Total for Question 19 = 4 marks)

A busy weekend

B

20 What did these people do last weekend? Read the following sentences:

A Got ready for a competition.	**E** Played some musical instruments.
B Went shopping for clothes.	**F** Took the dog out for a walk.
C Celebrated a friend's anniversary.	**G** Went to the sports centre.
D Bought a birthday present.	

Put a cross in the **four** correct boxes.

	A	B	C	D	E	F	G
Example: Esteban					X		
(i) Juanita							
(ii) José							
(iii) Andrea							
(iv) Francisco							

(Total for Question 20 = 4 marks)

TV programmes

 Television

G   21 Read José's list of favourite TV programmes.

las noticias

dibujos animados

telenovelas

documentales

películas de terror

> Look out for cognates. These will help you understand the meaning of the words.

What is on his list? Put a cross in the **four** correct boxes.

Example: horror films	A sports programmes	B cartoons
X		
C quiz shows	D documentaries	E the news
F music concerts	G soaps	H adverts

(Total for Question 21 = 4 marks)

 TV programmes

D   22 Listen to Marisa talk about television programmes. Fill in the spaces with the appropriate word from the box below.

Example: Marisa particularly likes .....*adventure programmes*............................. .

(i)   She spends most of her time watching ....

(ii)   She hates ....

(iii)   She never watches ....

(iv)   She says soaps are ....

sports programmes	soaps	adventure programmes	boring	interesting
films	documentaries	rubbish	reality TV	

(Total for Question 22 = 4 marks)

Cinema

A trip to the cinema

D 23 Read this blog about Josefina's recent trip to the cinema.

> El sábado pasado fui al cine con mi novio, Esteban. Vimos la película *Siempre a su lado*, una película dramática estadounidense.
> Cuenta una historia real muy curiosa. Trata de un profesor japonés y de su leal perro, que siempre le esperaba enfrente de la estación de trenes.
> Un día, el dueño del perro no se presenta en la estación y el perro se queda esperando durante diez años. Recomendaría la película, aunque me hizo llorar.
> ¿Sabéis que hace unos años en Japón hicieron una estatua del perro?
> ¡Increíble!
> Josefina

Put a cross in the **four** correct boxes.

Example: Josefina went to the cinema last Saturday.	X
A Josefina went to the cinema with her neighbour.	
B Josefina saw a Canadian film.	
C The film was based on a true story.	
D Josefina thought the story was strange.	
E Josefina found the teacher unusual.	
F One of the main characters was a dog.	
G The story was ten years old.	
H Josefina thought the film was sad.	

(Total for Question 23 = 4 marks)

An interview with Antonio Banderas

A 24 Sara is talking about her recent interview with the actor Antonio Banderas. Answer the following questions **in English.**

  1 How does she describe the now famous actor? .... **(1 mark)**

  2 **(i)** Why didn't he fulfill his dream to become a professional footballer?

        .... **(1 mark)**

     (ii) Why is he so surprised at his most recent acting success?

        .... **(1 mark)**

  3 **(i)** Which type of characters does he prefer to play, or do voiceovers for?

        .... **(2 marks)**

     (ii) What does he most dislike about his current life?

        .... **(1 mark)**

  4 **(i)** Why does he feel unsettled? .... **(1 mark)**

     (ii) What does he miss? .... **(1 mark)**

(Total for Question 24 = 8 marks)

Had a go ☐   Nearly there ☐   Nailed it! ☐

Music

 Music

B 25 Read the blog entries from a discussion about music.

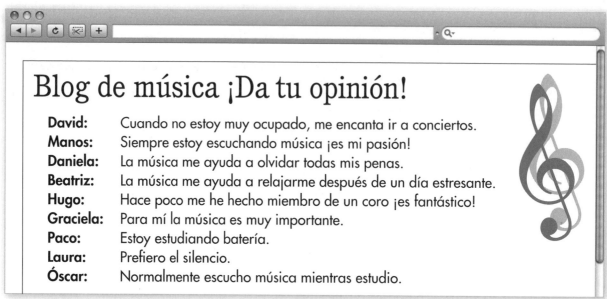

Blog de música ¡Da tu opinión!

David:	Cuando no estoy muy ocupado, me encanta ir a conciertos.
Manos:	Siempre estoy escuchando música ¡es mi pasión!
Daniela:	La música me ayuda a olvidar todas mis penas.
Beatriz:	La música me ayuda a relajarme después de un día estresante.
Hugo:	Hace poco me he hecho miembro de un coro ¡es fantástico!
Graciela:	Para mí la música es muy importante.
Paco:	Estoy estudiando batería.
Laura:	Prefiero el silencio.
Óscar:	Normalmente escucho música mientras estudio.

Who says the following? Write the correct name in the table below.

Example: Music is important for me.	Graciela
(i) Music helps me to forget.	
(ii) I love singing.	
(iii) I have music lessons.	
(iv) Music helps me to relax.	

(Total for Question 25 = 4 marks)

 Juan Zelada, musician

A* 26 Listen to this person talking about an interview he has had with Juan Zelada.
Answer the questions below **in English**.

1 Why does Juan say he is here? .... **(1 mark)**

2 What does he say about

   a) breakfast? .... **(1 mark)**

   b) his music? .... **(1 mark)**

3 What does he usually do

   a) in the mornings? .... **(1 mark)**

   b) in the evenings? .... **(1 mark)**

4 Why does he say he doesn't sleep? .... **(1 mark)**

5 What does he do once every week? .... **(1 mark)**

6 Why does he do this? .... **(1 mark)**

(Total for Question 26 = 8 marks)

Online activities

An evening on the internet

27 Read this blog about free time and the internet.

> ¿Qué puedes hacer si eres joven y estás aburrido? Para mí, Internet ofrece la solución ideal. Es rápido y fácil, y puedes hacer todo desde tu casa. Éstas son mis ideas para hacer actividades seguras con el ordenador.
>
> Para empezar, están las películas. Los fines de semana solía ir mucho al cine, pero ahora bajo películas de Internet y no salgo de casa. Es más barato y además se pueden leer las opiniones de los que las han visto antes de escoger una. Algunos padres creen que los videojuegos son una pérdida de tiempo, pero no es verdad. Jugar puede ser no solo divertido, sino también educativo. Algunos videojuegos te hacen pensar mucho.
>
> Otra ventaja es poder ver las noticias. Incluso los jóvenes necesitamos saber lo que pasa en el mundo. Hay muchas páginas web con noticias al minuto e información sobre gente famosa y cotilleos interesantes.
>
> Me gusta usar Internet para comunicarme con mis amigos, pero ofrece muchas más posibilidades. Por ejemplo, hace poco he empezado a estudiar francés y a aprender a tocar la guitarra.
>
> Marta

Answer the following questions **in English**.

1   What does Marta ask you at the start of her blog?

.... **(1 mark)**

2   Mention **two** things she says that describe her views on the internet.

....

.... **(2 marks)**

3   What does she say about downloading films from the internet? Mention **two** ideas.

....

.... **(2 marks)**

4   What does she say about the news?

.... **(1 mark)**

5   Apart from contacting friends, what else does Marta do? Mention **two** ideas.

....

.... **(2 marks)**

(Total for Question 27 = 8 marks)

For higher grade questions you will need to look out for different tenses and there may be words you don't know. Don't waste time worrying about these. Instead, look at the words around them to help you get a gist of what is being said. Often in reading comprehensions the questions can help direct you to the type of answer required.

Daily routine

 Óscar's routine

E 28 Read this e-mail from Óscar.

> | Borrar | Responder | Responder a todas | Adelante | Imprimir |
>
> ¡Hola!
>
> Hoy es lunes y como siempre, me desperté temprano, a las seis y cuarto, para ir al colegio. Primero me lavé los dientes y después me puse unos vaqueros. Como hacía buen tiempo, decidí ir al cole a pie. Esta tarde intentaré relajarme porque, por una vez, no tengo deberes.
>
> Óscar

Complete the box below **in English**.

Example: Day	......Monday..
(i) Wake up time	.... (1 mark)
(ii) Morning routine	.... (1 mark)
(iii) Travel to school	.... (1 mark)
(iv) Evening activities	.... (1 mark)

(Total for Question 28 = 4 marks)

 A typical morning

C 29 Listen to Roque talk about a typical school day. Fill in the gaps in the text below using an appropriate word or phrase from the box.

school	gets dressed	has breakfast	baths	packs his bag
does his homework		early	late	exercises

Example: Roque is talking about a typical ....school.................. day.

(i) He gets up .... during the week.

(ii) First he showers and ....

(iii) After that he ....

(iv) On the way to school he ....

(Total for Question 29 = 4 marks)

> Using logic can sometimes help you get to the answer. In this case, you wouldn't have a bath on the way to school so you know this isn't an option.

Breakfast

What's for breakfast?

G   **30** Which breakfast foods are listed below?

Put the correct letter beside each item.

Example: magdalenas	A
(i) cereales	
(ii) tostadas	
(iii) huevos	
(iv) jamón	

(Total for Question 30 = 4 marks)

Healthy eating

D   **31** Alba is reading a healthy living article. What does she say?
Listen and put a cross in the four correct boxes.

Example: Breakfast is important.	X
A Breakfast does not have a marked effect on health.	
B Alba is not surprised by the article.	
C Breakfast prepares you for anything.	
D The article discusses the advantages of breakfast.	
E It tells you the effects of not having breakfast.	
F It tells you what to eat.	
G Alba is not convinced.	
H Alba is going to change her ways.	

(Total for Question 31 = 4 marks)

Eating at home

Food preferences

C 32 Read what these people say about eating at home.

Isabel
Para mí, la comida más rica es la del domingo. Siempre tomamos chuletas o costillas, que para mí tienen que estar muy hechas. ¡Mi padre, sin embargo, las come casi crudas! La comida que más me gusta de todo el año es la comida navideña.

Gustavo
Yo prefiero la comida casera de mi padre. Hace platos deliciosos con especias e ingredientes exóticos. ¡En mi casa nos gusta lo picante!

Sofía
¡Lo que a mí me molan son los postres! Me encantan los helados, las tartas y todo tipo de pastelería, ¡aunque sé que no son nada buenos para la salud!

Match the people with their food preferences. Put a cross in the **four** correct boxes.

Likes	Isabel	Gustavo	Sofía
Example: Christmas dinner	X		
(i) tasty food			
(ii) fast food			
(iii) vegetarian food			
(iv) meat dishes			
(v) healthy dishes			
(vii) not so healthy dishes			
(viii) sweet dishes			

(Total for Question 32 = 4 marks)

Favourite food

F 33 Listen. What do they like to eat?

A	B	C	D	E	F
salad	pizza	fish	meat	omelette	chips

Put the correct letter next to each name.

Example: Artur	B
(i) Dolores	
(ii) Paco	
(iii) Loli	
(iv) Jorge	

(Total for Question 33 = 4 marks)

Keeping fit and healthy

 Keeping fit and healthy

A

34 Read this article about maintaining a healthy lifestyle

Todos sabemos que es necesario beber mucha agua durante el día para sentirse mejor porque ayuda con la digestión y es muy buena para la piel.

Por otra parte, también es importante comer una buena variedad de comida sana con mucha fruta y verduras, evitando la sal y la grasa.

Para tener una vida sana lo más importante no es tener una actitud positiva sino saber relajarse e identificar y solucionar los problemas que causan el estrés.

Para las personas que disfrutan del ejercicio físico vale la pena emplear a un especialista que les prepare un programa específico.

A mi juicio levantarse y acostarse temprano son más beneficiosos que obsesionarse con pasar un mínimo de ocho horas en la cama.

What **four** recommendations are made to maintain a healthy lifestyle? Put a cross in the **four** correct boxes.

Example: Drinking water	X		
A Getting up early		**E** Going for walks	
B Regular exercise		**F** Personal training	
C Balanced diet		**G** Avoiding stress	
D Sufficient sleep		**H** Positive attitude	

(Total for Question 34 = 4 marks)

 Keeping fit

Look at the activities and think how these might be said in Spanish before you hear the recording. You will then be better prepared.

35 Who wants to do what? Listen and put a cross in the correct box.

	A … go to the gym.	**B** … join a leisure centre.	**C** … play in a school team.	**D** … walk to school.	**E** … be in a dance club.	**F** … eat healthy food.
Example: Inés	X					
(i) Avelina						
(ii) Alfonso						
(iii) Carolina						
(iv) Juan						

(Total for Question 35 = 4 marks)

19

Health problems

Staying healthy

36 Read this article about healthy lifestyles.

> Es un hecho bien conocido que para llevar una vida sana es imprescindible mantenerse en forma haciendo ejercicio a diario. Ahora mucha gente tiene un entrenador personal para ayudarles con su régimen y con los ejercicios, pero la verdad es que no hace falta y puede salir bastante caro. Hacer un análisis simple de tu rutina diaria te puede ofrecer soluciones que no cuestan ni dinero ni tiempo. Por ejemplo, acostarte más temprano cada noche para pasar un rato leyendo y relajándote puede traer un beneficio considerable. Al levantarte, deja tiempo para dar un paseo corto por el jardín o por tu calle.
>
> A pesar de lo que dicen muchos, un poco de estrés no es algo totalmente negativo, lo que sí es importante es mantener una actitud positiva. Sugiero que hables con tu familia y amigos sobre lo que te preocupa, antes de que se convierta en un problema.
>
> Comer bien es otra cosa importante. No pasa nada por tomar comida rápida, mientras no lo hagas todos los días y sigas una dieta equilibrada. Se supone que una bebida alcohólica de vez en cuando no te puede perjudicar, pero debes evitar fumar a toda costa.
>
> Es muy importante beber, por lo menos, dos vasos grandes de agua al día y tomar suficientes frutas y verduras.

What **four** recommendations are made about maintaining a healthy lifestyle? Put a cross in the **four** correct boxes.

Example: regular exercise	X
A getting up early	
B revising your daily routine	
C avoiding fast food	
D reading	
E walking	
F personal training	
G talking to friends	
H drinking less alcohol	

> At this level it is important not to guess what the answer could be unless you are really stuck. Go through the text carefully and identify those activities you **do** understand.

(Total for Question 36 = 4 marks)

The body

 Health problems

C 37 Read these tweets.

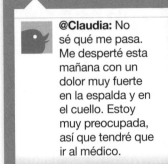

@Claudia: No sé qué me pasa. Me desperté esta mañana con un dolor muy fuerte en la espalda y en el cuello. Estoy muy preocupada, así que tendré que ir al médico.

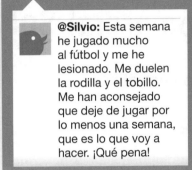

@Silvio: Esta semana he jugado mucho al fútbol y me he lesionado. Me duelen la rodilla y el tobillo. Me han aconsejado que deje de jugar por lo menos una semana, que es lo que voy a hacer. ¡Qué pena!

@Carmela: Acabo de volver de la playa y no me encuentro nada bien. Creo que tengo una insolación. Mi madre se va a volver loca. Me avisó que me pasaría eso y me temo que tenía razón.

Who says what? Put a cross in the **four** correct boxes:

	Claudia	Silvio	Carmela
Example: Has a sporting injury.		X	
(i) Is going to seek advice.			
(ii) Is following advice.			
(iii) Hasn't followed advice.			
(iv) Isn't sure what has happened.			

(Total for Question 37 = 4 marks)

 Young people and smoking

C 38 Some young people are talking about cigarettes. Read the statements.

A I hate the smell in the house.
B My parents say no to smoking.
C My parents are indifferent.
D Sporty people get short of breath.
E Smoking makes me ill.
F All my friends smoke, so I do too.
G Cigarettes are very expensive.

Listen. Write the correct letter in each box.

Example: Rafa	C
(i) Claudia	
(ii) Fabio	
(iii) Katia	
(iv) Navarro	

(Total for Question 38 = 4 marks)

At the tourist office

The shopping centre

E 1 Read the following advertisement for a shopping centre.

> # Centro comercial Sol y Sombra
>
> Nuevo centro comercial con:
>
> • Cien tiendas
> • Aparcamiento gratis
> • Horario de apertura: de 10:00 a 20:00 cada día; cerrado los domingos
> • A tres kilómetros del centro de la ciudad
> • Gran variedad de cafeterías y restaurantes
> • Cinco salas de cine
> • Prohibido fumar en todas partes

Answer the following **in English**. Full sentences are not required.

(i)   How many shops are there? ....

(ii) On which day of the week is the centre closed? ....

(iii) How far is the centre from the town centre? ....

(iv) What are you not allowed to do at the centre? ....

(Total for Question 1 = 4 marks)

Deciding what to do

B 2 Lucía's parents are discussing where to go. Why do they choose Isla Mágica?
Listen and put a cross in the **four** correct boxes.

A there is a direct train there	
B it isn't expensive	
C it opens late	
D how close it is to Barcelona	
E the variety of activities	X
F it's extremely popular	
G the number of different restaurants	
H the night life	
I the weather	

(Total for Question 2 = 4 marks)

What to do in town

What to do in town

3 Read Rodrigo's opinions about things to do in town.
What does he like to do? Put a cross in the **four** correct boxes.

Example: Me encanta visitar castillos.	X
A No me gusta ir al cine.	
B Ir de compras es interesante.	
C Dar un paseo por el parque es bueno para la salud.	
D ¿Ir a la piscina ? ¡No gracias!	
E Comer en un restaurante es caro.	
F Jugar al fútbol es mi actividad preferida.	
G Ir al mercado es aburrido.	
H Ir al teatro es divertido.	

> Look out for **negative** phrases with likes and dislikes.

(Total for Question 3 = 4 marks)

Going out in town

4 Who wants to do what? Listen and put a cross in the correct box.

	A I want to go shopping.	**B** I want to go to the theatre.	**C** I want to go to the museum.	**D** I want to go to the park.	**E** I want to go ice skating.	**F** I want to go to the cinema.
Example: Elena	X					
(i) Sara						
(ii) Julio						
(iii) Amina						
(iv) Serena						

(Total for Question 4 = 4 marks)

23

Signs in town

Tourist information

F   5   Read these signs.

A

Casa Marco
Restaurante italiano
Calle Principal, 155

B

Biblioteca municipal
Horario: 9:00 – 18:00

C

Centro de ocio
Gimnasio, piscina

D

Supermercado Max
a 200 metros de aquí

E

Peluquería Dedo
Abre todos los días excepto
los lunes

F

Tienda de recuerdos
Ideas para toda la familia

Match where the people wish to go with the signs above and put a cross in the correct box.

	A	B	C	D	E	F
Example: Grace wants an Italian meal.	X					
(i) Paco wants to buy food.						
(ii) Julia is going swimming.						
(iii) Luca needs to borrow a book.						
(iv) Amelia is looking for presents.						

(Total for Question 5 = 4 marks)

In the town

E   6   Which sign is each of these people talking about?

A	B	C	D	E	F
Town centre	No smoking	Car park	No dogs	Exit	Station

Put a cross in the correct box.

	A	B	C	D	E	F
Example:			X			
(i)						
(ii)						
(iii)						
(iv)						

(Total for Question 6 = 4 marks)

At the train station

At the train station

G

7   Look at the signs you would find at a train station.

A

> Left luggage 🧳

B

> Platform

C

> Waiting room

D

> Exit

E

> Information ⓘ

F

> Toilets 🚺🚹

Match the following words with the correct picture.

Example: información	E
(i) la consigna	
(ii) los servicios	
(iii) el andén	
(iv) la salida	

(Total for Question 7 = 4 marks)

At the railway station

F

8   Where do these people need to go?

A

> Exit ➡

B

> Café

C

> Left luggage 🧳

D

> Platform

E

> Timetable

F

> Waiting room

Listen and put the correct letter in the boxes below.

Example:	B
(i)	
(ii)	
(iii)	
(iv)	

> Use the reading time to think about the words you are likely to hear.

(Total for Question 8 = 4 marks)

Weather

 Weather

E 9 Read the following entries about the weather.

> **Título:** El clima
>
> **Antonio:** Me encanta el sol.
>
> **María:** Cuando llueve, me quedo en casa.
>
> **Jesús:** Me encanta la nieve, porque me gusta mucho esquiar.
>
> **Isabel:** Cuando hace buen tiempo se puede dar una vuelta en bici.
>
> **Martín:** Cuando hace frío no puedo salir al jardín.

What are they writing about?

A sunny weather   **C** stormy weather   **E** cold weather

B fine weather   **D** rainy weather   **F** snowy weather

Put a cross in the correct box.

	A	B	C	D	E	F
Example: Antonio	X					
(i) María						
(ii) Jesús						
(iii) Isabel						
(iv) Martín						

(Total for Question 9 = 4 marks)

 Holiday weather

E 10 Listen to these young people talking about the weather. Which weather are they talking about?

A	B	C	D	E	F
snow	rain	sun	wind	storm	cold

Put a cross in the correct box.

	A	B	C	D	E	F
Example:			X			
(i)						
(ii)						
(iii)						
(iv)						

(Total for Question 10 = 4 marks)

Places in a town

Juan's holiday

Ⓖ **11** What is on the list?

Example: castillo
(i) cine
(ii) museo
(iii) piscina
(iv) playa

> Many of these words are cognates. Do the ones you know first, then concentrate on those you are unsure of.

Put a cross in the **four** correct boxes.

Example: castle	**A** market	**B** beach
X		
C supermarket	**D** church	**E** swimming pool
F cinema	**G** park	**H** museum

(Total for Question 11 = 4 marks)

Going places

Ⓖ **12** Listen to the tourists. Where do they want to go?

A	**B**	**C**	**D**	**E**	**F**
supermarket	leisure centre	station	library	shopping centre	bakery

Listen and put the correct letter in the grid below.

Example:	C
(i)	
(ii)	
(iii)	
(iv)	

(Total for Question 12 = 4 marks

Where I live

 My town

C

13 Read these tweets.

@Carmen: Mi ciudad es ideal para los que disfrutan del deporte. Sin embargo, mis amigos y yo no tenemos mucho que hacer. Han cerrado el cine y no hay club de jóvenes.

@Santi: He vivido al lado del mar durante diez años. Es genial. Los fines de semana en verano son fantásticos porque la ciudad está muy animada. Lo único malo es que en invierno todo está cerrado.

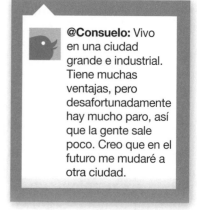
@Consuelo: Vivo en una ciudad grande e industrial. Tiene muchas ventajas, pero desafortunadamente hay mucho paro, así que la gente sale poco. Creo que en el futuro me mudaré a otra ciudad.

Who says what? Put **four** crosses in the correct columns.

	Carmen	Santi	Consuelo
Example: The place is good for sport.	X		
(i) Is thinking about moving away.			
(ii) Says it depends on the season.			
(iii) There is little to do where they live.			
(iv) Says people don't go out much.			

(Total for Question 13 = 4 marks)

 My home town

A

14 Listen to Bernardo talking about his home town. Answer the following questions **in English**.

Part A

(i) How does Bernardo describe where he lives in Gran Canaria? .... **(1 mark)**

(ii) What does he say is good about it? .... **(1 mark)**

(iii) What does he say about the people who live there? .... **(1 mark)**

(iv) Name one of the disadvantages of living there. .... **(1 mark)**

Part B

(i) Where will Bernardo take his penfriend? Name **two** places.

.... **(2 marks)**

(ii) What is special about the place he will take him to eat? .... **(1 mark)**

(iii) Why will Bernard's friend like it there? .... **(1 mark)**

(Total for Question 14 = 8 marks)

Town description

Memories of my town

15 Read this article.

Yo había pasado una infancia bastante normal y corriente en mi pueblecito del norte de Chile, hasta el tremendo acontecimiento del día cinco de agosto de dos mil diez. Me acordaré siempre de mi tío Félix que volvía cada día de la mina San José, donde trabajaba, y decía que un desastre estaba al caer. Y así fue. Ese día se derrumbó la mina y se quedaron atrapados treinta y tres hombres, incluyendo a mi tío. Yo estaba desesperada y pensaba que se iba a morir. Afortunadamente, después de sesenta y nueve días bajo tierra salieron todos vivos, la mayoría sin heridas graves. A mi tío le tuvieron que operar los dientes, pero nada más. Estoy muy agradecida porque sobrevivió y también porque no piensa bajar a la mina nunca más. A pesar de lo difícil que es encontrar trabajo por aquí, José ha conseguido un puesto como mecánico en Copiapó. ¡Menos mal!

Answer the questions **in English**.

(a) What overall impression does this girl give of her childhood?

.... **(1 mark)**

(b) What did her uncle always talk about?

.... **(1 mark)**

(c) Why was he right?

.... **(1 mark)**

(d) What happened to the men?

.... **(1 mark)**

(e) What does she say about employment in her region?

.... **(1 mark)**

(f) Why is she relieved? Give **two** reasons.

(i) .... **(1 mark)**

(ii) .... **(1 mark)**

(g) What has happened to her uncle since?

.... **(1 mark)**

(Total for Question 15 = 8 marks)

You don't need to answer in full sentences, but do make sure your answer is clear.

Holiday destinations

Where do they like to go?

D 16 Where do these people like to go on holiday? Read what they say.

Marta	A mí me gusta la ciudad.
Enrique	A mí me gusta la playa, pero para hacer deporte, no para tomar el sol.
Luisa	Me encanta viajar y, si es posible, a sitios exóticos.
Manuel	Lo que necesito es relajarme y para eso, el campo siempre me parece la mejor opción.
Clara	Como me encanta esquiar, prefiero ir a las montañas.

Put a cross in the correct box.

	A countryside	B beach	C campsite	D exotic place	E city	F mountains
Example: Marta					X	
(i) Enrique						
(ii) Luisa						
(iii) Manuel						
(iv) Clara						

(Total for Question 16 = 4 marks)

Holiday destinations

G 17 Where do they prefer to go on holiday?

A	B	C
mountains	coast	theme park

D	E	F
island	campsite	countryside

Listen and put a cross in the correct box.

	A	B	C	D	E	F
Example:		X				
(i)						
(ii)						
(iii)						
(iv)						

(Total for Question 17 = 4 marks)

Holiday accommodation

Where to stay

B 18 Read these opinions.

Pili	Me encantan los hoteles. Me gusta no tener que hacer mi cama ni ayudar en nada. Allí hay gente que te lo hace todo. ¡Es genial!
Pablo	Me gustan las actividades al aire libre. Soy una persona sencilla y no necesito muchos lujos.
Maruja	Lo que a mí me gusta es poder hacer mis deportes preferidos, tengo un kayak y me gusta nadar largas distancias. Es muy difícil hacerlos en la ciudad donde vivo.
Juli	No soy aficionado a las vacaciones en hoteles. Prefiero pasar mis vacaciones en casa de familia y amigos.

Complete these sentences with the correct name.

Example: ....Pili............ likes hotels.

(a) .... likes watersports.

(b) .... doesn't like to be indoors.

(c) .... doesn't like work.

(d) .... cares more about who to spend a holiday with.

> Watch out for the negative expressions such as *no ... ni.*

(Total for Question 18 = 4 marks)

Holiday accommodation

D 19 Listen to these young people talking about their holidays.
Where do they stay? Put a cross in the correct box.

	cousin's house	hotel	city flat	tent	camp site	youth hostel
Example: Marcelo			X			
(i) Paulina						
(ii) Rogelio						
(iii) Samuel						
(iv) Eva						

(Total for Question 19 = 4 marks)

Staying in a hotel

Hotel feedback

C 20 Read the comments.

¿Qué piensas de tu hotel?

Marcelo: Nuestra habitación estaba muy limpia y era cómoda. Daba gusto.
Benjamín: Mi mujer no durmió durante todas las vacaciones debido al ruido.
Sofía: En el hotel la comida era muy buena. Había mucha variedad y cosas para todos los gustos.
Fátima: El hotel tenía piscina, sala de juegos y una lavandería. Era de cuatro estrellas.
Julen: La verdad es que era muy caro nuestro hotel.

What aspect of the hotel accommodation is mentioned by each person?

A	B	C	D	E	F
locality	cleanliness	cost	food	sleep quality	facilities

Put a cross in the correct box.

	A	B	C	D	E	F
Example: Marcelo		X				
(i) Benjamín						
(ii) Sofía						
(iii) Fátima						
(iv) Julen						

(Total for Question 20 = 4 marks)

Staying in a hotel

C 21 Some young people are talking about holiday accommodation. Read the statements.

A I always stay full board.
B I have to have a balcony.
C I am only interested in a sea view.
D I prefer a room with a shower.
E I need a half board deal.
F I like to reserve online.
G I only stay in five star hotels.

Listen and write the correct letter in each box.

Example: Rafa	B
(i) Claudia	
(ii) Francisco	
(iii) Nuria	
(iv) Nacho	

(Total for Question 21 = 4 marks)

Staying on a campsite

Camping

D

22 Read this e-mail from Federico.

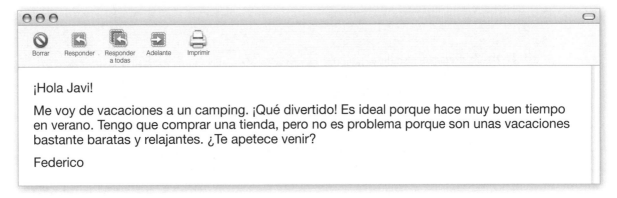

¡Hola Javi!

Me voy de vacaciones a un camping. ¡Qué divertido! Es ideal porque hace muy buen tiempo en verano. Tengo que comprar una tienda, pero no es problema porque son unas vacaciones bastante baratas y relajantes. ¿Te apetece venir?

Federico

Put a cross next to the **four** things he mentions about camping.

Example: It is fun.	X
A You can do it anywhere.	
B It is very popular.	
C The weather in summer is good.	
D It is very uncomfortable.	
E You need transport to do it.	
F You need to buy the right equipment.	
G It is relaxing.	
H It is cheap.	

(Total for Question 22 = 4 marks)

Camping holiday

C

23 Ana is talking about a recent camping trip. What does she say? Listen and put a cross in the **four** correct boxes.

> This passage will be in the past tense. Make sure you have revised all those irregular forms.

Example: I had a good time.	X
A It rained a lot.	
B It was my first camping trip.	
C There was lots to do.	
D The tents were small.	
E The beds were uncomfortable.	
F The campsite was noisy.	
G It was cold at night.	

(Total for Question 23 = 4 marks)

Holiday preferences

Holiday preferences

24 Read this article about holiday preferences.

> **Juan:** Yo creo que irse de vacaciones es una idea estupenda, pero preferiría ir después de los exámenes del colegio. Como ya tengo dieciséis años, preferiría pasar las vacaciones con mis amigos en vez de con mis padres, como de costumbre. Así que, a partir del diez de junio me vendría bien porque mi amigo Carlos tiene el último examen el día anterior. Es bastante difícil decidir dónde ir porque somos seis. Todos quieren ir a Grecia, pero yo no estoy tan seguro. Creo que hará demasiado calor.
>
> **María:** No me interesa para nada irme de vacaciones con mis amigos. Dentro de tres meses cumplo dieciocho años, pero no tengo ganas de estar lejos de mi familia, como muchos jóvenes. De hecho, pienso pasar mis vacaciones este año con mis hermanas. La semana que viene vamos a ir juntas a una agencia de viajes para organizar un viaje de tres semanas a México. Es el momento ideal, ya que de momento, mi tío está trabajando allí. Si no aprovechamos esta oportunidad será una pena, porque en casa de mi tío no tenemos que pagar alojamiento.

Put a cross in the **four** correct boxes.

Example: Juan está deseando irse de vacaciones.	X
A Juan y María quieren viajar con sus amigos.	
B Juan todavía no ha decidido adónde ir.	
C A Juan le gusta pasar las vacaciones al sol.	
D Juan y María quieren ir de vacaciones al extranjero.	
E A María le preocupa lo que va a costar.	
F Juan y María van a celebrar su cumpleaños.	
G María va a reservar sus vacaciones la semana que viene.	
H Juan y María están preocupados por los exámenes.	

(Total for Question 24 = 4 marks)

Deciding where to go

25 Chus and Gorka talk about their holiday preferences. Which suggestions do they make? Listen and put a cross in the **four** correct boxes.

	Chus	Gorka
Example: a one-week holiday	X	
A coach travel		
B night life		
C air travel		
D watersports		

(Total for Question 25 = 4 marks)

Holiday activities

 On holiday

F 26 Read this holiday advert.

Ofrecemos actividades para todos:

A equitación
B esquí acuático
C sala de juegos
D piscina cubierta
E clases de baile

Which activities do these people choose? Write the correct letter in each box.

Example: Mario Me gustan los deportes acuáticos.	(i) Felicia Me gusta el ballet.	(ii) Santiago Me encanta nadar.
B		
(iii) Daniela Me encantan los caballos.	**(iv) Quique** Me gusta jugar al ping-pong.	

(Total for Question 26 = 4 marks)

 A typical holiday

D 27 Carlos is describing a typical holiday.
Listen and put a cross in the correct box to finish each sentence.

Example: Carlos went on holiday with his …

A girlfriend.	
B family.	X
C friends.	

(i) He spent most days …

A in the bar.	
B in the games room.	
C at the pool.	

(ii) He had dinner …

A at home.	
B in the hotel.	
C out.	

(iii) In the afternoons he went …

A cycling.	
B horse riding.	
C rollerblading.	

(iv) If the weather was bad they went …

A horse riding.	
B skating.	
C bowling.	

(Total for Question 27 = 4 marks)

Booking accommodation

A camping holiday

  28 Read the letter.

> Estimado señor:
>
> El año pasado pasamos una semana maravillosa en su camping. Como sé que se llena rápidamente en temporada alta, le escribo para solicitar una reserva durante dos semanas a finales de julio o principios de agosto. Queremos todo igual que la vez anterior.
>
> ¿Nos podría ofrecer un sitio más cerca de la piscina este año? Está cerca de todo lo demás y podríamos vigilar a los niños sin tener que bañarnos todo el rato.
>
> Como vamos en coche, también necesitamos reservar un espacio para aparcar, y además pensamos llevar al perro. ¿Sería eso posible? ¿Costaría más?
>
> Muchas gracias.
>
> Saludos cordiales,
>
> Gregorio Ferrer

> At A grade you will be expected to be able to recognise past, present and future tenses. These could all affect the answer, so make sure you revise your verb forms.

Answer the questions **in English**.

(a) Why are these tourists returning to the campsite?

.... **(1 mark)**

(b) How long does the family plan to stay at the campsite?

.... **(1 mark)**

(c) Why are they contacting the campsite so soon?

.... **(1 mark)**

(d) (i) Where do they want their pitch to be?

.... **(1 mark)**

(ii) Why? Give **two** reasons. ....

.... **(2 marks)**

(e) What **two** special enquiries do they make?

....

.... **(2 marks)**

(Total for Question 28 = 8 marks)

Future holiday plans

 A planned holiday

A **29** Read what Nuria has planned to do during her holiday.

A	**Sábado:**	Ya he quedado con mis amigos en pasar el día relajándonos tomando el sol y jugando en la arena. Tengo muchas ganas de tomar un helado y pasar un rato con un buen libro.
B	**Domingo:**	Iré a misa en la iglesia antigua y después iré a ver el acueducto y el ayuntamiento del siglo catorce. Estoy deseando ver todos los sitios que he estudiado.
C	**Lunes:**	No puedo pasar mis vacaciones sin visitar la famosa fábrica de perlas. Será el lugar ideal para comprar regalos. También quiero ver recuerdos típicos y los vinos de la región.
D	**Martes:**	Como quiero aprender a cocinar comida típica y casera, he reservado una plaza en el curso de cocina del gran hotel Félix. Sé que volveré a casa sabiendo preparar unas recetas estupendas.
E	**Miércoles:**	Pasaré la mayor parte del día lavando y planchando ropa y ordenando mis cosas. Tendré que pasar todo el día haciendo la maleta para el viaje de vuelta.
F	**Jueves:**	¡No quiero ni pensarlo! Todo se habrá terminado y estaré rumbo a casa. ¡Qué pena!

Match each activity with the correct day in the grid below.

Example: packing	F
(i) sightseeing	
(ii) classes	
(iii) beach	
(iv) shopping	

(Total for Question 29 = 4 marks)

 Next summer

C **30** Inés is going on holiday. Listen to what she says. Write the appropriate letter to complete the sentences below.

A	**B**	**C**	**D**	**E**
sailing	walking	family	eating	riding

F	**G**	**H**	**I**	**J**
hotel	pool	sightseeing	friends	flat

Example: Inés is going with her ......C........ .

(i) They will stay in a ....

(ii) In the mornings she will go ....

(iii) In the afternoons she will go ....

(iv) Inés plans to spend the evenings ....

(Total for Question 30 = 4 marks)

Past holidays

My summer holiday

31 Read this e-mail from Guillermo.

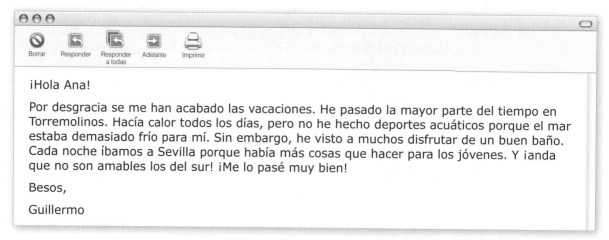

¡Hola Ana!

Por desgracia se me han acabado las vacaciones. He pasado la mayor parte del tiempo en Torremolinos. Hacía calor todos los días, pero no he hecho deportes acuáticos porque el mar estaba demasiado frío para mí. Sin embargo, he visto a muchos disfrutar de un buen baño. Cada noche íbamos a Sevilla porque había más cosas que hacer para los jóvenes. Y ¡anda que no son amables los del sur! ¡Me lo pasé muy bien!

Besos,

Guillermo

What does Guillermo say? Put a cross in the **four** correct boxes.

Example: The holiday is now over.	X
A He spent less than a fortnight in Torremolinos.	
B On certain days, the weather wasn't warm.	
C Everyone found the sea water too cold to swim in.	
D Some people went swimming in the sea.	
E On just one occasion they visited Seville.	
F Seville offered activities for people of Guillermo's age.	
G The local people were friendly.	
H The holiday experience was pleasant.	

(Total for Question 31 = 4 marks)

Holiday memories

32 Listen to Raquel talking about her childhood holidays. Put a cross next to the **four** correct statements.

Example: Raquel stayed with her grandmother.	X
A She stayed in the city.	
B The location was very noisy.	
C Raquel enjoyed outdoor pursuits.	
D The accommodation was luxurious.	
E She never went on holiday alone.	
F She stayed for a few days.	
G She has fond memories of these holidays.	
H She remembers the sights and sounds.	

(Total for Question 32 = 4 marks)

Directions

 Directions

G **33** Look at the symbols. Which directions do they relate to?

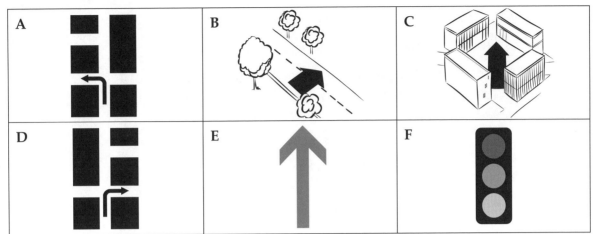

Find the right sign for each direction. Write the correct letter in each box.

Example: Pase el semáforo.	F
(i) Toma la primera calle a la izquierda.	
(ii) Cruza la plaza.	
(iii) Sigue todo recto.	
(iv) Gira a la derecha.	

(Total for Question 33 = 4 marks)

 Finding the way

F **34** Where do they have to go?

A	B	C	D	E	F
Turn left.	Straight ahead.	Go up the road.	Take the first right.	Cross the square.	Pass the bridge.

Put a cross in the correct box.

	A	B	C	D	E	F
Example:		X				
(i)						
(ii)						
(iii)						
(iv)						

(Total for Question 34 = 4 marks)

Had a go ☐ Nearly there ☐ Nailed it! ☐

Transport

 Public transport

 35 Read Guillermo's letter.

> Querido amigo:
>
> Me preguntas por los autobuses en mi ciudad.
> Pues el servicio no me parece muy bueno. Los
> billetes cuestan mucho y los viajes duran
> bastante. Por ejemplo, un viaje en coche hasta el
> centro solo dura unos quince minutos, mientras
> que en autobús es por lo menos media hora.
>
> Normalmente los asientos son cómodos, pero el
> problema es que no hay suficientes, y a menudo
> hay que estar de pie. Los viajes nocturnos
> pueden ser ruidosos.
>
> ¡Odio viajar en autobús!
>
> ¡Hasta pronto!
>
> Guillermo

> Make sure you have
> revised vocabulary such
> as *hasta*, *a menudo* and
> *por lo menos*. These are
> used regularly in Spanish
> and will affect the
> answer.

Put a cross in the correct box to complete each sentence.

Example: Guillermo is writing about local ...

(i)	buses.	X
(ii)	trains.	
(iii)	coaches.	

(a) Travelling by bus is ...

(i)	expensive.	
(ii)	good value.	
(iii)	cheap.	

(b) Travelling by bus is ...

(i)	boring.	
(ii)	slow.	
(iii)	complicated.	

(c) There are generally ...

(i)	enough seats.	
(ii)	plenty of seats.	
(iii)	too few seats.	

(d) Night buses are sometimes ...

(i)	noisy.	
(ii)	dangerous.	
(iii)	cold.	

(Total for Question 35= 4 marks)

Buying tickets

Travelling

B

36 Read this blog.

El transporte

¿Cómo llegas tú?

Mario:	Voy a todas partes en mi bici.
Loli:	Es una barbaridad lo que cuestan los aparcamientos.
Kiko:	No uso el tren, porque la estación está a una hora de mi casa.
Laura:	Siempre voy a pie porque es muy sano y barato.
Eduardo:	Mi vecino es taxista, ¡algo muy conveniente para mí!
Margot:	Lo que cuesta no es importante, lo importante es el efecto en el medio ambiente.
Patricio:	Me molesta mucho que ningún autobús pase por mi casa.
Sara:	Viajar en autobús por mi ciudad es muy cómodo y barato.
Tito:	Hay demasiados coches, lo que contribuye a unos atascos impresionantes.

Who says what? Write the correct name in the table.

Example: I use my bicycle.	Mario
(a) I can't use public transport because I live too far away.	
(b) I hate traffic jams.	
(c) I am happy to use public transport.	
(d) The cost of parking is too high.	

(Total for Question 36 = 4 marks)

Interrailing

A

37 Pepe and Ana are discussing their recent trip around Europe. Write down four advantages and disadvantages in English.

Advantages	Disadvantages
1	1
2	2
3	3
4	4

(Total for Question 37 = 8 marks)

> Listen carefully when it is more than one person speaking. They may have different opinions on the same thing and you will need to identify this.

Eating tapas

An e-mail

E

1   Read Ana's e-mail.

> ¡Hola!
> ¿Qué tal?
> Acabo de estar en una nueva heladería. Es bastante original y hay un ambiente agradable.
> Hay mucha variedad en el menú, pero cuesta mucho. Van muchos jóvenes y eso me gusta.
> Creo que volveré allí en el futuro.
> Manolo

Choose the correct words from the list to complete the sentences.

expensive	different	clothes	ice cream	limited
cakes	varied	Manolo	cheap	pleasant

Example: It's an e-mail from ..... Manolo ....

(i)   The café's speciality is ....

(ii) Manolo found the atmosphere ....

(iii) The menu was ....

(iv) The cost of the food was ....

(Total for Question 1 = 4 marks)

What do they want to eat?

G

2   What do these people want to eat?

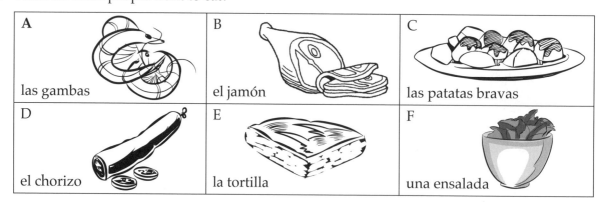

	A	las gambas
B	el jamón
C	las patatas bravas
D	el chorizo
E	la tortilla
F	una ensalada

Listen and put a cross in the correct box.

	A	B	C	D	E	F
Example:					X	
(i)						
(ii)						
(iii)						
(iv)						

(Total for Question 2 = 4 marks)

Eating in a café

In the café

F 3 What do they order?

A Chus

Quiero una limonada.

B Elvira

Me apetece un zumo de naranja.

C Juan

Para mí, agua sin gas.

D Fátima

Yo quiero un té con limón.

E Nando

Voy a tomar un café con leche.

Put a cross in the correct box to show what each person ordered.

	A Chus	B Elvira	C Juan	D Fátima	E Nando
Example: lemonade	X				
(i) still water					
(ii) white coffee					
(iii) orange juice					
(iv) tea with lemon					

(Total for Question 3 = 4 marks)

Buying drinks

F 4 Listen to these young people. What drinks did they order? Put a cross in the **four** correct boxes.

	A herbal tea	B Coca-Cola	C orange juice	D black coffee	E glass of milk	F cup of tea
Example:		X				
(i)						
(ii)						
(iii)						
(iv)						

(Total for Question 4 = 4 marks)

You can see the answers will refer to 'things', so concentrate on the **nouns** while you listen.

Eating in a restaurant

 Eating out

C   **5**   Read what people say about eating out.

> **¿Por qué comes fuera?**
>
> **Marga:** Porque me gusta experimentar y probar sabores diferentes.
> **Alejandro:** Normalmente solo salgo a cenar si hay alguna fiesta o algo parecido.
> **Juan:** Comer fuera te ahorra mucho tiempo.
> **Carmen:** No disfruto nada cocinando y tampoco me hace gracia tener que hacer la compra primero.
> **Ricardo:** Me gusta comer y charlar con gente porque es muy relajante.

What does each person refer to? Put a cross in the **four** correct boxes.

A new things	**D** social benefits
B food preparation	**E** cost
C time saving	**F** celebrations

	A	B	C	D	E	F
Example: Juan			X			
(i) Marga						
(ii) Alejandro						
(iii) Carmen						
(iv) Ricardo						

(Total for Question 5 = 4 marks)

 Eating in a restaurant

D   **6**   Listen to the dialogue. Put a cross in the correct box.

Example: The number of people is …

A four.	X
B five.	
C six.	

(i) They want to sit …

A indoors.	
B on the terrace.	
C in the garden.	

(ii) They choose to sit there because

A it's raining.	
B it's hot.	
C it's cold.	

(iii) There's a special daily menu …

A at lunch times.	
B all day.	
C in the evenings.	

(iv) 30 euros will buy you …

A one course.	
B two courses.	
C three courses.	

(Total for Question 6 = 4 marks)

Opinions about food

Food and drink

D   7   What do they like to eat and drink?

María	Me gusta tomar té.
Raúl	Creo que el pollo está muy rico en un sándwich, pero no lo como nunca con verduras.
Laura	Nunca tomo bebidas calientes, como té o café. Los zumos me parecen demasiado dulces y normalmente solo tomo agua.
Mikel	Como cualquier cosa con verduras, pescado o queso, pero nada de carne.
Clara	Sé que debería tomar mucha fruta y verduras, pero odio las dos cosas. Si me dejan elegir, ¡prefiero tomar tarta!

Put a cross in the correct box.

	A cake	B tea	C vegetables	D water	E juice	F chicken
Example: María		X				
(i) Raúl						
(ii) Laura						
(iii) Mikel						
(iv) Clara						

(Total for Question 7 = 4 marks)

Favourite food

C   8   Mimi, Iago and Raquel are talking about their preferences. Who says the following?
Listen and put a cross in the correct box.

	Mimi	Iago	Raquel
Example: I love Italian food.	X		
(i) I'd rather eat fast food.			
(ii) I don't eat meat.			
(iii) I hate spicy food.			
(iv) I love seafood.			

(Total for Question 8 = 4 marks)

Restaurant problems

Restaurant feedback

C 9   Read this letter of complaint.

> Estimado señor:
>
> Cené en su restaurante el sábado pasado y no quedé nada contenta.
>
> Para empezar, reservé una mesa en la terraza para seis personas, pero al llegar nos ofrecieron una mesa para cuatro en un rincón oscuro al lado de la cocina.
>
> Tuvimos que esperar media hora en el bar antes de poder cenar, y cuando por fin llegó la comida, estaba fría.
>
> El servicio fue muy lento. El camarero trajo vino blanco, en vez de vino tinto, y se le olvidaron por completo nuestros postres.
>
> Debido a todos esos problemas, pienso que pagamos demasiado.
>
> Por último, le puedo asegurar que no pienso recomendar su restaurante a nadie.
>
> Quedo a la espera de su respuesta.
>
> Atentamente,
>
> Rocío Rodríguez

What are the facts? Put a cross in the **four** correct boxes.

Example: Rocío went out on Saturday.	X
A Rocío arrived late.	
B The table was inside.	
C The food was cold.	
D The restaurant was recommended.	
E The service was poor.	
F The waiter forgot their drinks.	
G The meals were expensive.	

> Some sentences may appear at first glance to be correct. Make sure you read through the text carefully and don't assume the answer.

(Total for Question 9 = 4 marks)

An evening out

B 10 Alejandro, Nadia and Marta are discussing a recent meal they had out. Who says the following? Put a cross in the correct box.

	A Alejandro	B Nadia	C Marta
Example: The meal was expensive.	X		
(i) The food was cold.			
(ii) The service was slow.			
(iii) The restaurant was too noisy.			
(iv) The waiter was rude.			

(Total for Question 10 = 4 marks)

Shops

 Town centres

 11 Read this article.

¡Caen como moscas!

Una preocupación del gobierno actual es la progresiva desaparición en algunos lugares de España de los centros de comercio históricos dentro de las ciudades. Pero ¿cuáles son las razones? En realidad, hay muchas.

El aumento de las compras por Internet hace la vida muy difícil para los pequeños negocios y tiendas. Además de unas ganancias más reducidas, los dueños tienen que pagar el alquiler de sus locales y así es muy difícil competir con las empresas que venden por Internet.

Los clientes están cada vez menos dispuestos a pagar los aparcamientos, que son bastante caros. Prefieren comprar desde sus hogares. Es más cómodo y, sobre todo, resulta más barato.

Con la intención de cambiar esta tendencia, el gobierno ha anunciado una serie de medidas diseñadas para revitalizar los centros de comercio históricos de las ciudades.

En primer lugar, van a hacer una encuesta a todos los habitantes para averiguar qué piensan que hay que hacer.

En segundo lugar, están organizando transporte gratis desde los aparcamientos en las afueras de la ciudad hasta los centros de comercio históricos, así la gente podrá aparcar y no sufrirá la congestión del tráfico.

Por último, van a poner más policías de servicio para bajar la delincuencia.

Si quiere más información o está interesado en ayudar, contacte con nuestro centro de información llamando al 00 76 39 20 20.

Lo que está claro es que si no hacemos algo ahora, los centros de comercio de nuestras ciudades van a desaparecer para siempre.

Answer the questions **in English**.

(a) According to the article, why are town centres dying? Give **two** details.

.... **(2 marks)**

(b) Why is online shopping so popular these days? Give **two** details.

.... **(2 marks)**

(c) What is the government proposing to do to improve town centre shopping?
Give **two** details.

.... **(2 marks)**

(d) What should you do if you are interested in these projects?

.... **(1 mark)**

(e) What will happen if we don't take action?

.... **(1 mark)**

(Total for Question 11 = 8 marks)

Had a go ☐   Nearly there ☐   Nailed it ☐

Shopping for food

At the supermarket

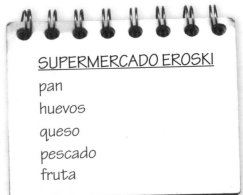

SUPERMERCADO EROSKI

pan

huevos

queso

pescado

fruta

G **12** What is on the list? Put a cross in the **four** correct boxes.

Example:	A	B
X		
C	**D**	**E**
F	**G**	**H**

(Total for Question 12 = 4 marks)

A shopping list

C **13** Susana is going shopping. What does she need? Read the list.
Listen and put a cross in the **four** correct boxes.

Example: a loaf of bread	X
(a) 250 grams of cheese	
(b) a dozen eggs	
(c) four bananas	
(d) a kilo of sugar	
(e) a small packet of rice	
(f) two bottles of lemonade	
(g) a large box of biscuits	
(h) a tin of sardines	
(i) a small chicken	

(Total for Question 13 = 4 marks)

At the market

 Buying presents

F **14** What is Rafael buying? Write the correct letter in the grid below.

A	B	C
a doll	a rucksack	a box of chocolates

D	E	F
flowers	a pen	a belt

Example:	Para mi madre, bombones.	C
(i)	Mi abuelo quiere un bolígrafo.	
(ii)	A Nuria le encantaría una muñeca.	
(iii)	Para Conchi, como siempre, flores.	
(iv)	Por último, un cinturón para mi hermano.	

(Total for Question 14 = 4 marks)

 At the market

F **15** What are they buying? Listen and put a cross in the most appropriate box.

	A is buying melon.	B plans to make a salad.	C is buying fruit.	D is a meat eater.	E needs vegetables.
Example: Sebastian	X				
(i)					
(ii)					
(iii)					
(iv)					

(Total for Question 15 = 4 marks)

> Food words in Spanish are often cognates, but make sure you know how these are said as sometimes they sound quite different from the English.

Signs in shops

In a department store

B   **16** Read this review.

El Corte Inglés – Lo que piensa un visitante de Venezuela – Rodrigo Pérez

"Durante mis últimas vacaciones entré en El Corte Inglés por primera vez, y para mí fue una sorpresa agradable. Lo que más me impresionó fue que todo se encontraba fácilmente, desde las ofertas especiales hasta las cestas, ¡algo muy importante si no tienes mucho tiempo, o si eres extranjero como yo! Se ve desde lejos donde están todas las cosas, desde los ascensores hasta las salidas, pero lo que más me gustó fue la zona de rebajas, donde anunciaban descuentos de hasta un cincuenta por ciento. Pasé una hora fantástica allí. Me gustaron mucho el diseño y los productos. ¡Todo muy fácil! ¡Desde luego volveré algún día!"

Rodrigo

What does the reviewer say about El Corte Inglés? Put a cross in the **four** correct boxes.

Example:	Rodrigo went there for the first time.	X
A	He found everything easy to locate.	
B	He was interested in the sale area.	
C	He says you need lots of time.	
D	He found discounts of up to 50%.	
E	There was 40% off some products.	
F	He used the lifts and toilets.	
G	He wasn't impressed by the design or products.	
H	It was a positive experience for him.	

(Total for Question 16 = 4 marks)

A shop announcement

D   **17** Listen to this announcement about a special offer. Answer the questions **in English**.

(a) What are customers being informed about?

.... **(1 mark)**

(b) When will they be open tomorrow?

.... **(1 mark)**

(c) When will they be open again after that?

.... **(1 mark)**

(d) What happens on that day?

.... **(1 mark)**

(Total for Question 17 = 4 marks)

Clothes and colours

Talking about fashion

B 18 Read these opinions.

Patri	Me encanta la moda. Trabajo en una tienda de ropa que vende cosas fabulosas. Tengo un descuento en las cosas que compro. ¡Es genial!
Paco	Me gusta la moda, pero prefiero no gastar mucho dinero en ropa, así que a menudo compro en tiendas de segunda mano. ¡Es muy divertido!
Marina	Me gusta ser diferente, así que compro mi ropa cuando voy al extranjero. Así siempre tengo algo original.
Juan	No soy aficionado a la ropa ni a la moda. Prefiero la ropa cómoda, como la de deporte. Los chándales y las zapatillas son lo que más me pongo.

Complete these sentences with the correct name.

Example: .....Juan................. likes sportswear.

(a) .... buys second-hand clothes.

(b) .... is not interested in fashion.

(c) .... buys clothes abroad.

(d) .... can buy discounted items.

(Total for Question 18 = 4 marks)

Buying clothes

G 19 Listen to these young people talking about clothes. What do they want?

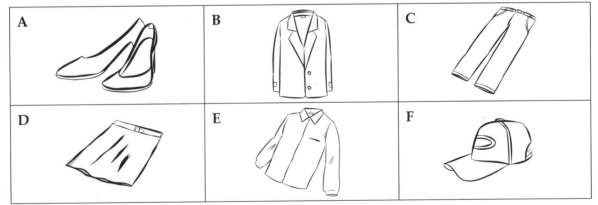

Put a cross in the correct box.

	A	B	C	D	E	F
Example:				X		
(i)						
(ii)						
(iii)						
(iv)						

(Total for Question 19 = 4 marks)

Shopping for clothes

The clothes party

C 20 Read the email below. Is the opinion positive or negative? Put a cross in the correct box.

Borrar Responder Responder a todas Adelante Imprimir

¡Hola Sofía!

Anoche fui a la fiesta de ropa en casa de Ángela. Me gustó porque estaba entre amigos.

Vimos la ropa y había mucha variedad, aunque los precios eran un poco caros. La ropa estaba bien hecha y además, era de tela ecológica.

Lo malo es que era muy difícil probarse cosas porque no había espejos.

Vale la pena ir, ¡te gustará!

Besos,

Julia

> This text is quite short so you will need to understand most of the vocabulary in order to get the right answers.

	Party aspect	Positive opinion ☺	Negative opinion ☹
Example:	the venue	X	
(i)	the clothes		
(ii)	the quality		
(iii)	the prices		
(iv)	the changing facilities		

(Total for Question 20 = 4 marks)

A dress for the prom

B 21 Angela is buying a dress for the Prom. What reasons does she give for her choice?
Put a cross in the **four** correct boxes.

	Example: The dress is blue.	X
A	The dress has a belt.	
B	The dress has short sleeves.	
C	The dress is fashionable.	
D	The dress is not too long.	
E	The dress is original.	
F	The dress is in the sale.	
G	The dress has a matching bag.	
H	The dress fits well.	

(Total for Question 21 = 4 marks)

Returning items

 Returns

 22 Why are these people returning items?

Mario
No me gusta.

David
Es demasiado grande.

Julieta
No funciona.

Daniela
Está roto.

Paquito
No es mi talla.

Put a cross in the correct box.

	Mario	Daniela	David	Julieta	Paquito
Example: doesn't like it	X				
(i) It is the wrong size.					
(ii) It is too big.					
(iii) It is broken.					
(iv) It doesn't work.					

(Total for Question 22 = 4 marks)

 A problem at the shop

23 Susi has a problem with some trousers. Listen and complete the sentences using the most appropriate ending.

A damaged	B have her money back	C in the car
D in the office	E the wrong size	F yesterday
G this evening	H exchange the trousers	I tomorrow

Write the **four** correct letters in the boxes below.

Example: Susi bought the trousers [F] .

(i) She is complaining because the trousers are [ ] .

(ii) She would like to [ ] .

(iii) She left her receipt [ ] .

(iv) She wants to wear the trousers [ ] .

(Total for Question 23 = 4 marks)

Online shopping

 Shopping online

 24 What does this website sell?

A	Libros	D	Música: CD y DVD
B	Juegos	E	Equipamiento deportivo
C	Ropa	F	Todo para la casa

Put the correct letter in the table below.

Example: CDs	D
(i) games	
(ii) clothes	
(iii) books	
(iv) sports equipment	

(Total for Question 24 = 4 marks)

 46 Online shopping

A **25** Listen. What do these young people say about online shopping?

A You could risk losing your money.

B There are some good bargains.

C I never shop online.

D I don't have time to shop.

E Home delivery can be a problem.

F I always use companies I know well.

> Read the questions first and try to work out what you'll hear in Spanish.
>
> Listen to the example – it tells you each person will speak separately.

Write the correct letter in the box.

Example: Elvira	D
(i) Vicente	
(ii) Olivia	
(iii) Simón	
(iv) Begoña	

(Total for Question 25 = 4 marks)

Shopping opinions

Shopping trends

C

26 Read what these people say about shopping.

Elvira

No entiendo por qué a la gente le gusta ir de compras. Yo prefiero quedarme en casa y comprar por correo. A veces, sin embargo, compro cositas en la tienda que está al lado de mi casa porque es más práctico.

Antonia

Yo no soy aficionada a comprar. Sin embargo, me gusta estar a la moda. Últimamente muchos de mis amigos hacen fiestas para vender de ropa y maquillaje y eso me gusta. ¡Ganan dinero también!

Pepito

Normalmente compro en las tiendas de uno de los centros comerciales que hay en Burgos. Me encanta la variedad y suelen ser más baratos. ¡Es la mejor manera de comprar! De vez en cuando también compro por Internet.

Put a cross in the **four** correct boxes in the grid to show who talked about the items in the first column.

	Elvira	**Antonia**	**Pepito**
Example: the internet			X
(i) party sales			
(ii) local shops			
(iii) shopping centres			
(iv) mail order			

(Total for Question 26 = 4 marks)

Shopping preferences

D

27 Ana, Pedro and Inés are discussing shopping preferences. Who says the following? Listen and put a cross in the correct columns.

	Ana	**Pablo**	**Inés**
Example: I love shopping.		X	
(i) I don't mind large shopping centres.			
(ii) I don't like local shops.			
(iii) I prefer window shopping.			
(iv) I like to shop from catalogues.			

(Total for Question 27 = 4 marks)

Travelling

Rail travel

A* 28 Read this article.

Los problemas de los trenes

A pesar de todos los avances tecnológicos, viajar en tren todavía puede resultar problemático. Aquí damos una lista de los problemas principales y de algunas soluciones posibles:

Problema: A veces los trenes paran largo rato sin ninguna explicación.

Solución: En estos casos, lo único que se puede hacer es tener paciencia.

Problema: Los trenes tardan más que otros medios de transporte, como los aviones.

Solución: Si necesitas llegar a algún sitio a una hora determinada, calcula por lo menos una hora extra de tiempo por si hay retraso. Si eso no te parece bien, utiliza otro método de transporte.

Problema: Puede resultar difícil comprar un billete de tren para una hora punta, incluso si lo compras por adelantado.

Solución: Si estás seguro de las fechas del viaje que quieres hacer, procura comprar tu billete con antelación, y mejor resérvalo por Internet o por teléfono. Las largas colas en la estación podrían hacer que llegues tarde o que pierdas el tren.

Problema: Para llegar a la estación, normalmente hay que utilizar otro medio de transporte, excepto si vives cerca.

Solución: Cómprate una bicicleta. Son baratas y se pueden llevar en el tren.

Problema: Llevar tu equipaje de un sitio o vehículo a otro puede resultar un inconveniente.

Solución: Planifica con anticipación. Llama a un taxi, pide que te llegue a una hora concreta y te llevará justo hasta la estación. Si no, podrías pedir a un amigo que te lleve.

What are the problems and solutions? Complete the grid **in English** ensuring that the solution corresponds with the problem.

Problem	Solution
Example: Breakdowns	Be patient.
(i)	**(i)**
(ii)	**(ii)**
(iii)	**(iii)**
(iv)	**(iv)**

(Total for Question 28 = 4 marks)

Train travel

E 29 Your Spanish friend is buying a train ticket. Complete the form in **English.**

Example: Destination ...... Madrid ......

(a) Day: ....

(b) Problem: ....

(c) How many tickets: ....

(d) Price €: ....

(Total for Question 29 = 4 marks)

56

Travel problems

 A bus journey

D 30 Read this blog about Antonia's recent bus journey.

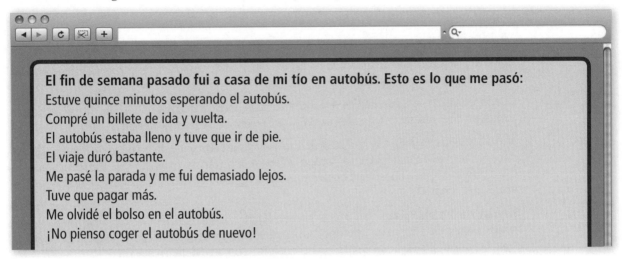

El fin de semana pasado fui a casa de mi tío en autobús. Esto es lo que me pasó:

Estuve quince minutos esperando el autobús.

Compré un billete de ida y vuelta.

El autobús estaba lleno y tuve que ir de pie.

El viaje duró bastante.

Me pasé la parada y me fui demasiado lejos.

Tuve que pagar más.

Me olvidé el bolso en el autobús.

¡No pienso coger el autobús de nuevo!

Put a cross in the **four** correct boxes.

Example: Antonia was visiting her uncle.	X
A The bus was late.	
B Antonia waited for a quarter of an hour.	
C Antonia bought a return ticket.	
D Antonia chose to stand.	
E The bus was crowded.	
F The journey was fast.	
G Antonia got off at the wrong stop.	
H Antonia's bag was stolen.	

(Total for Question 30 = 4 marks)

 At the train station

C 31 Carmen is talking about catching the train. What does she like? What doesn't she like?

A price	**C** staff	**E** crowds	**G** proximity
B cleanliness	**D** safety	**F** delays	**H** canteen

Write the **four** correct letters in the table.

☺	☹

(Total for Question 31 = 4 marks)

Money problems

Looking after your money

32 Read this letter Santi's grandmother has written to him.

> Mi querido Santi:
>
> Como ahora que estás estudiando no tienes dinero, te mando veinte euros. Con ellos puedes abrir una cuenta en el banco.
>
> Bueno, y no sólo eso, además te voy a contar algo horrible que me pasó. Fue anteayer, me atacaron en el mercado. Me caí al suelo y me tuvieron que llevar al hospital.
>
> No pasó nada grave. Estoy bien ahora, solo muy asustada y me da un poco de miedo salir de casa. La verdad es que fui tonta porque llevaba mucho dinero conmigo. ¡Me robaron cien euros! Ojalá que no te pase nunca una cosa semejante. Esto me ha hecho pensar y te aconsejo que abras una cuenta.
>
> Es muy importante porque así mantendrás seguro tu dinero. Además, lo bueno es que hoy en día te dan un regalito, como un teléfono móvil o descuentos especiales, por ejemplo. Por supuesto tendrás que demostrar tu identidad porque sin eso, no te dejaran abrirla.
>
> Por último, te recuerdo que la cuenta debe ser principalmente para cuidar tu dinero. ¡No te endeudes!
>
> ¡Qué te lo pases bien… y no gastes mi dinero de golpe!
>
> Abuelita Graciosa

Part A

Answer the following questions **in English**.

(i) What happened to Santi's grandmother in the market?

.... **(1 mark)**

(ii) How is she now? .... **(1 mark)**

(iii) Why does she blame herself? .... **(1 mark)**

(iv) What does she advise Santi? .... **(1 mark)**

Part B

Write **two** advantages and **two** disadvantages of opening a bank account according to Santi's grandmother.   **(4 marks)**

Advantages	Disadvantages
(i)	**(i)**
(ii)	**(ii)**

(Total for Question 32 = 8 marks)

> Look carefully at the number of marks given for each answer and make sure you write down the appropriate number of points.

58

Lost property and theft

A text message

33 Read David's message.

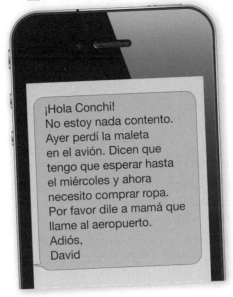

¡Hola Conchi!
No estoy nada contento.
Ayer perdí la maleta
en el avión. Dicen que
tengo que esperar hasta
el miércoles y ahora
necesito comprar ropa.
Por favor dile a mamá que
llame al aeropuerto.
Adiós,
David

Answer the following questions **in English.**

(i) What has David lost? .... **(1 mark)**

(ii) Where did this happen? .... **(1 mark)**

(iii) When will David get this item back? .... **(1 mark)**

(iv) What does David have to do now? .... **(1 mark)**

(v) What does David want Conchi to do? .... **(1 mark)**

(Total for Question 33 = 4 marks)

A street crime

34 Andrea is reporting a robbery. Answer the following questions **in English.**

(a) When did the robbery happen? .... **(1 mark)**

(b) What was stolen? .... **(1 mark)**

(c) What exactly happened? Give **two** details. ....

.... **(2 marks)**

(d) What did the thief look like? Give **two** details. ....

.... **(2 marks)**

(e) (i) What details does Andrea give about the handbag?

.... **(1 mark)**

(ii) What is Andrea asked to do?

.... **(1 mark)**

(Total for Question 34 = 8 marks)

Complaints and problems

A delivery problem

B 35 Read the letter.

> 6 de mayo de 2012
>
> Muy señor mío:
>
> Me dirijo a usted para quejarme de un grave error por parte de su empresa.
>
> La semana pasada compré unos libros muy necesarios para mis estudios ya que tengo un examen la semana que viene. Me aseguraron que llegarían al día siguiente, y no solo eso, también me dijeron que sería a primera hora de la mañana y que no tendría que pagar más por eso.
>
> Pedí tiempo libre en el trabajo para estar en casa y recibir el paquete, pero no apareció nadie. Más tarde, cuando volví del trabajo, había una nota diciendo que habían intentado entregarlo ¡a las cuatro de la tarde!
>
> Me gustaría saber lo que piensa hacer para rectificar este error y compensarme.
>
> Espero con interés su respuesta.
>
> Atentamente,
>
> Celestina Gómez

Complete the sentences using the most appropriate letter from the list.

Example:	Celestina has some	C
(i)	She expected delivery	
(ii)	Celestina wasted her	
(iii)	She received	
(iv)	She wants	

A	an answer.
B	books.
C	exams.
D	by hand.
E	money.
F	time.
G	before 10am.
H	a note.

(Total for Question 35 = 4 marks)

Problems

C 36 Begoña, Fabio, Lupe and Urbano had problems on a recent trip abroad. Who mentions what? Write the name of the correct person.

Begoña	Fabio	Lupe	Urbano

Example: .....Fabio............. missed the train.

(a) .... lost some ID.

(b) .... ran out of money.

(c) .... needed medical attention.

(d) .... had a bag stolen.

(Total for Question 36 = 4 marks)

School subjects

 School subjects

F 1 Which subjects do they prefer? Put the correct letter in each box.

A los deportes	**C** las lenguas	**E** la geografía
B las ciencias	**D** el teatro	**F** la música

Example:	Me gusta jugar al fútbol.	A
(i)	Me encanta la biología.	
(ii)	Mi asignatura favorita es el inglés.	
(iii)	Toco la guitarra.	
(iv)	Quiero ser actriz.	

> Make sure you know the various ways of saying you like something in Spanish. It isn't always going to be *Me gusta*.

(Total for Question 1 = 4 marks)

 School

G 2 Listen to these young people talking about school subjects. What do they like to study?

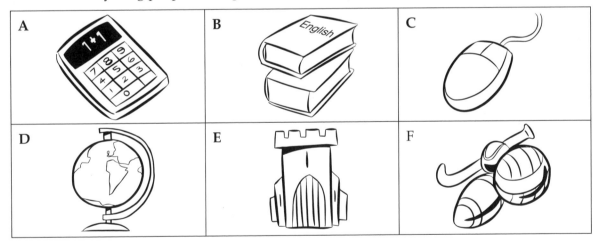

Put a cross in the correct box.

	A	**B**	**C**	**D**	**E**	**F**
Example:			X			
(i)						
(ii)						
(iii)						
(iv)						

(Total for Question 2 = 4 marks)

School description

Back to school

G   3   Which items are on sale? Put a cross in the **four** correct boxes.

> bolígrafos
> gomas
> sacapuntas
> reglas
> cuadernos

Example:	A	B
X		
C	D	E
F	G	H

(Total for Question 3 = 4 marks)

Learning English

E   4   Javier is talking about his English lessons. Listen to the dialogue. Put a cross in the correct box.

Example: Javier's lesson is on …

A Monday.	
B Wednesday.	X
C Friday.	

(i) Javier's class is …

A small.	
B mixed.	
C noisy.	

(ii) They mainly do …

A reading.	
B speaking.	
C writing.	

(iii) Javier finds this subject …

A important.	
B fun.	
C easy.	

(iv) Javier says his teacher is …

A kind.	
B strict.	
C unusual.	

(Total for Question 4 = 4 marks)

School routine

A typical school day

Ⓒ

5 Read what people say about their school day.

¿Qué piensas de tu colegio?

Susana: Es un buen colegio, pero los profesores ponen demasiados deberes.

Tere: Las clases duran demasiado.

Arantxa: Todos los días tenemos muchas actividades después del colegio.

Lucas: Hay demasiadas reglas que hay que respetar.

Mikel: Hay mucha variedad de cosas que se pueden estudiar.

What does each person refer to? Put a cross in the correct box.

A timetable	C extra curricular activities	E exams
B curriculum	D homework	F discipline

	A	B	C	D	E	F
Example: Susana				X		
(i) Tere						
(ii) Arantxa						
(iii) Lucas						
(iv) Mikel						

(Total for Question 5 = 4 marks)

A typical day

Ⓓ

6 Listen to Andrés describing a typical school day. Put a cross in the correct box.

Example: Andrés is talking about …

A Monday.	
B Tuesday.	X
C Wednesday.	

(i) Andrés got to school …

A on time.	
B late.	
C early.	

(ii) His first lesson was …

A Maths.	
B English.	
C Science.	

(iii) He finds this subject …

A important.	
B fun.	
C useful.	

(iv) At lunch time he …

A revised for a test.	
B went home.	
C talked to his friends.	

(Total for Question 6 = 4 marks)

Comparing schools

My school exchange

D

7 Read this blog about Rafaela's recent school exchange trip.

> Hace poco pasé una semana en Inglaterra en un intercambio. Esto es lo que descubrí:
> Estudian física y química como nosotros.
> Allí juegan mucho al fútbol.
> Tienen más deberes que en mi cole.
> Estudian sólo un idioma extranjero.
> Les gusta la informática.
> Llevan uniforme.
> Todos los días comen en el comedor del cole.

Put a cross in the **four** correct boxes.

Example: Rafaela spent a week at the school.	X
A She was ill most days.	
B They study science.	
C They do sport too.	
D They study more than one language.	
E They are into ICT.	
F They don't have to do homework.	
G They can wear whatever they like.	
H They have lunch at school.	

(Total for Question 7 = 4 marks)

English schools

F

8 Listen to Conchi talking about a visit to an English school. What did she like? What didn't she like?

A the students	**D** the lessons	**G** the homework
B the uniform	**E** the food	**H** discipline
C the teachers	**F** the length of the school day	

Write the **four** correct letters in the table.

	🙂	☹
Example: B		
	(i)	(i)
	(ii)	(ii)

(Total for Question 8 = 4 marks)

At primary school

My old school

D

9 Read these opinions on primary schools.

Ana	Tenía muchos amigos.
Ricardo	Mis profesores siempre me ayudaban.
Rafa	Todos los veranos íbamos de excursión.
Marina	Me gustaban el inglés y las matemáticas.
Julia	Todos respetábamos las reglas.

> If you don't recognise some of these irregular verbs, concentrate on the rest of the sentence as this is where the answer can be found.

What does each person mention? Put a cross in the **four** correct boxes.

	Ana	Ricardo	Rafa	Marina	Julia
Example: school trips			X		
(i) staff					
(ii) subjects					
(iii) discipline					
(iv) friends					

(Total for Question 9 = 4 marks)

Primary school

C

10 Listen to some young people talking about their primary schools. Read the statements.

A My teacher knew me well.
B I liked languages and literacy the best.
C I liked mixed ability classes.
D The classes were small.
E We ate an apple every day.
F Our teachers made learning fun.
G Sport was optional.

Listen and write the correct letter in each box.

Example: Begoña	E
(i) Antonio	
(ii) Juanita	
(iii) Cesc	
(iv) Gerardo	

(Total for Question 10 = 4 marks)

School rules

School rules

Ⓒ 11 Read this letter from Martín.

¡Hola!

En mi colegio las cosas han cambiado. Ahora tenemos que llevar uniforme y dicen que el año que viene van a prohibir llevar pendientes y también anillos. Los profesores no son muy estrictos, pero no nos dejan usar el móvil. Los ordenadores son mejores y podemos usar el correo electrónico.

Todavía hay problemas con algunos alumnos que tiran basura y estudian poco, pero su comportamiento es mejor y en el cole ahora hay un ambiente agradable.

Saludos,

Martín

What were there rules about in the school before, what happens now, and what will happen in the future? Put a cross in the **four** correct boxes.

	Past	Present	Future
Example: uniform		X	
(i) jewellery			
(ii) mobile phones			
(iii) litter			
(iv) bullying			

(Total for Question 11 = 4 marks)

School life

Ⓒ 12 Listen to Íker, Carolina, Sergio and Cristina talking about school life. Who mentions what? Write the name of the correct person.

| Íker   Carolina   Cristina   Sergio |

Example: Who thinks behaviour is good? .....Carolina..........

(a) Who thinks there is too much litter? ....

(b) Who thinks lessons are noisy? ....

(c) Who is concerned about attendance? ....

(d) Who thinks academic standards are too low? ....

(Total for Question 12 = 4 marks)

Discussing the future

 My future plans

C

13 Read what these people say about their future plans. Put a cross in the **four** correct boxes in the grid below.

Marta

Creo que nos preocupamos demasiado por el futuro. Siempre hay tiempo para estudiar. Quiero pasar un año viajando por otros países antes de hacer los exámenes.

Maxi

Espero ir a la universidad. El futuro es muy importante para mí. Me encantan los idiomas y eso es lo que quiero estudiar. Primero necesito aprobar los exámenes. Dos años más en el cole, ¡no es demasiado!

Alberto

Encuentro el instituto bastante aburrido, pero tengo miedo de no poder conseguir un trabajo si no estudio. Lo ideal para mí sería trabajar y estudiar a la vez.

Who mentions …	Marta	Maxi	Alberto
Example: university		X	
(i) unemployment			
(ii) staying at school			
(iii) travelling			

(Total for Question 13 = 4 marks)

 My study choices

G

14 Listen to these young people talking about their study choices.
What do they plan to study next?

A		B		C	
D		E		F	

Put a cross in the correct box.

	A	B	C	D	E	F
Example:				X		
(i)						
(ii)						
(iii)						
(iv)						

(Total for Question = 4 marks)

Future plans

Future plans

A

15 Read the letter.

> ¡Hola Miguel!
>
> Acabo de terminar los exámenes y estoy agotada. No tenía ni idea de lo difícil que es repasar tantas cosas. Si saco buenas notas, voy a seguir estudiando. Espero ir a la universidad para hacer una carrera de idiomas – alemán o quizás inglés – todavía no estoy segura.
>
> Lo bueno de estar en la ciudad es que podré vivir con mis padres. Nos llevamos muy bien y me ayudarán con el coste de la vida universitaria. Podré estudiar y ahorrar a la vez, ¡qué guay! Hasta podré ir a pie y si no, me llevará mi padre en coche.
>
> En cuanto termine la universidad me gustaría buscar un trabajo en Londres porque dicen que la vida nocturna es genial y necesitaré un poco de relax. Cuando me respondas, avísame de lo que piensas hacer en septiembre.
>
> ¡Chao por ahora!
>
> Patricia

Complete the sentences. Choose the correct letter from the list.

Example: Patricia ha hecho ...	F
(i) A Patricia le pareció bastante duro …	
(ii) Patricia está segura de ...	
(iii) La vida en la universidad será ...	
(iv) Patricia quiere empezar ...	

A su vida profesional en Londres.

B francés y alemán.

C repasar tantas cosas.

D querer estudiar idiomas.

E fácil y divertido.

F unos exámenes en el colegio.

G más barata si se queda en casa.

(Total for Question 15 = 4 marks)

Future careers

C

16 Listen to some young people talking about their future careers. What is important for them? Put a cross in **four** boxes.

	Maite	**Íñigo**	**Borja**	**María**	**Jesús**
Example: travel	X				
(a) teamwork					
(b) being outdoors					
(c) having fun					
(d) money					

(Total for Question 16 = 4 marks)

Jobs

  Jobs

G 17 What jobs do they mention?

A Pilar

Mi padre es piloto.

C Ángela

Mi hermano es mecánico.

E Martín

Quiero ser profesor.

B Dolores

Soy camarera.

D Federico

Mi madre es enfermera.

Put a cross in the correct box.

	Pilar	Dolores	Ángela	Federico	Martín
Example: pilot	X				
(i) waiter					
(ii) nurse					
(iii) mechanic					
(iv) teacher					

(Total for Question 17 = 4 marks)

  My father's job

B 18 Inés is talking about her father's job. Read the questions. Put a cross in the correct boxes.

Example: He works in a ...

A hospital.	X
B kitchen.	
C bank.	

> Make sure you listen right to the end of the passage before you answer the questions. Listen out carefully for words such as *pero* (but).

(i) He finds his work ...

A tiring.	
B boring.	
C difficult.	

(ii) He travels to work ...

A by bus.	
B by car.	
C on foot.	

(iii) He prefers working with ...

A babies.	
B children.	
C older people.	

(iv) He finds the salary ...

A sufficient.	
B poor.	
C good.	

(Total for Question 18 = 4 marks)

Job adverts

Vacancies

F 19 Read this advert.

Centro comercial

Necesitamos:

A tres cocineros/as

B dependientes/as para varias tiendas

C enfermero/a con experiencia

D peluquero/a

E agentes de viaje

F camareros/as

Match the jobs to the people. Write the appropriate letter for each person.

María **Example:** Soy chef.	(i) Felipe Soy cajero.	(ii) Susana Corto el pelo.
A		
(iii) Daniel Trabajo en un hospital.	(iv) Kiko Organizo vacaciones.	

(Total for Question 19 = 4 marks)

A job advert

> Don't lose marks by giving too much information. Look carefully at the number of points you need to provide.

A* 20 Listen to this radio advert. Answer the questions below **in English**.

(i) When would the work start? .... **(1 mark)**

(ii) What type of work is on offer? .... **(1 mark)**

(iii) What is the prospective employer looking for in applicants? Name **two** things.

.... **(2 marks)**

(iv) What might make the job attractive to listeners? Name **two** things.

.... **(2 marks)**

(v) What would be the next step for prospective candidates? Name **two** things.

.... **(2 marks)**

(Total for Question 20 = 8 marks)

CV

Ana's CV

21 For each piece of text find the correct heading. Write the letter of the heading in the box.

A Idiomas	D Experiencia laboral
B Calificaciones	E Cualidades
C Fecha de nacimiento	F Referencias

(i)

He trabajado durante cinco años como traductora para varias editoriales internacionales. De momento tengo un contrato con Casa Alianza. Durante mis estudios tenía trabajillos.

(ii)

Acabo de terminar el Bachillerato y he hecho varios cursos de informática. Tengo carné de conducir y varias medallas de deporte.

(iii)

Adjunto una carta del director de mi instituto y una del jefe de mi empresa actual. Podría conseguir más referencias si hace falta.

(iv)

Soy una persona entusiasta, muy educado y con buena presencia. Tanto mis profesores del colegio, como mis jefes hablan bien de mí y de mis aportaciones en clase o en el trabajo.

(Total for Question 21 = 4 marks)

A good CV

22 Listen to this interview with Señor Alonso, director of a software company. Answer the questions below **in English.**

(i) Why, according to Señor Alonso, is it important to have a good CV?

.... (1 mark)

(ii) What does he say you should include? Name **two** things.

.... (2 marks)

(iii) What does he say you should be careful with? Name **two** things.

.... (2 marks)

(iv) What does he say about a one-fits-all CV?

.... (1 mark)

(v) What does he say you should do before starting to write your CV?

.... (1 mark)

(vi) How would this affect your CV? .... (1 mark)

(Total for Question 22 = 8 marks)

71

A job application

Applying for a job

B   **23** Read this letter. Answer the questions by putting a cross in the correct box.

> Muy señor mío:
>
> He visto su anuncio en el periódico local y le escribo para solicitar el puesto de dependienta en su tienda de ropa.
>
> Tengo mucho interés en semejante puesto porque me gustaría entrar en el sector del comercio. Hace poco acabé los estudios de secundaria y ahora busco un trabajo de verano antes de ir a la universidad en otoño. Hice mis prácticas de trabajo en una agencia de viajes y he tenido varios trabajillos en hoteles del vecindario.
>
> Como se puede ver en el currículum que le mando adjunto, destaco en las asignaturas de informática y empresariales, y además domino el francés y el inglés. Soy trabajadora, honrada y puntual. Estoy disponible para empezar inmediatamente.
>
> Espero atentamente su respuesta para concertar una entrevista.
>
> Un cordial saludo,
>
> Rosa Martínez

> Don't get daunted by longer texts. Start with the questions you can do easily then focus on the more difficult parts.

Example: This job was advertised ...

A nationally.	
B locally.	X
C privately.	

(i) Rosa will be working in ...

A a hotel.	
B a travel agent's.	
C a shop.	

(ii) Rosa wants to work ...

A at weekends.	
B in the holidays.	
C part time.	

(iii) Rosa did work experience in …

A a university.	
B a travel agent's.	
C a hotel.	

(iv) Rosa's skills include ...

A languages.	
B maths.	
C science.	

(Total for Question 23 = 4 marks)

Job interview

Preparing for an interview

A*

24 Read this article.

Los mejores consejos para tener éxito en una entrevista

En cualquier entrevista hace falta causar una buena impresión y demostrar que eres la mejor persona para el trabajo. ¡Sigue estos consejos y tendrás éxito!

A nadie le gusta que le hagan esperar, así que llega temprano a la entrevista y viste apropiadamente.

Al entrar en la habitación causarás una buena impresión si andas con confianza, no te encojas y da la mano con firmeza al presentarte.

Nunca te sientes antes de que te lo digan y acuérdate de sonreír educadamente. Sé amable y mira a tu entrevistador a los ojos.

Mantener el contacto visual con quien te habla cuando te entrevista demuestra que te interesa lo que dice. Recuerda hacer preguntas inteligentes si te dan la oportunidad de hacerlo.

Contesta cada pregunta ampliamente y no solo con

un 'sí' o un 'no'. Es muy importante dar ejemplos que demuestren tus habilidades y tus éxitos.

Habla bien claro. Pregunta si no entiendes o pide que repitan si no oyes bien. Y ante todo, recuerda ser honesto. Normalmente es obvio si alguien está mintiendo. Intenta ser positivo, mantente tranquilo y no te apartes de los hechos.

What should you do at interview? Complete the grid **in English.**

Do	Reason
Example: be on time	people don't like to wait
(i)	**(i)**
(ii)	**(ii)**
(iii)	**(iii)**
(iv)	**(iv)**

(Total for Question 24 = 8 marks)

An interview

E

25 Listen to a young person who is at a job interview. What does he say? Answer the following questions **in English**.

Example: Name: ......Ignacio..............................

(a) Age: ....

(b) Favourite subject: ....

(c) Personal quality: ....

(d) Start date: ....

(Total for Question 25 = 4 marks)

Opinions about jobs

A working day

B 26 Read this article.

> Me llamo Ronaldo y nací en Argentina, pero llevo cinco años trabajando en el barrio de Leganés, en Madrid. Mi esposa es madrileña. Para mí es mucho mejor trabajar aquí porque el transporte público es excelente y puedo ir en metro. Lo malo es que vivo bastante lejos, así que tengo que levantarme a las seis de la mañana. Soy enfermero y lo que más aprecio de mi trabajo es el contacto con la gente y trabajo en equipo. Sin embargo, suelo trabajar muchas horas y encuentro las tareas difíciles. La mayoría de los pacientes son amables y mis compañeros de trabajo también. A la hora de comer nos gusta ir a alguno de los bares de tapas de la zona. Madrid tiene fama por sus buenos restaurantes.

Put a cross in the **four** correct boxes.

Example: Ronaldo was born in Argentina.	X
A He likes to get to work early.	
B He travels to work by underground.	
C He enjoys working with people.	
D Ronaldo finds his job easy.	
E A disadvantage of his job is the long hours.	
F He doesn't get on well with his colleagues	
G The patients are generally unbearable.	
H Ronaldo usually leaves his work place at lunch time.	

(Total for Question 26 = 4 marks)

Looking for a job

B 27 Two friends are looking for a job. Which job do they select?
Listen and write a cross against the job they choose.

A activity leader		**B** hairdresser		**C** waiter	

Why? Put a cross for the **three** correct reasons.

A It's easy.	
B It pays well.	
C It's fun.	
D It's close to home.	
E They can work together.	
F It's something new.	
G You don't need experience.	

(Total for Question 27 = 4 marks)

Part-time work

A Saturday job

E

28 Read Ana's email.

> ¡Hola!
>
> ¿Qué tal? Trabajo en una tienda de moda. La jornada es demasiado larga. Empiezo a las ocho de la mañana y termino a las siete de la tarde. Tengo dos horas para comer y normalmente tomo un bocadillo con mis amigos. Me llevo bien con el jefe porque es divertido. Sólo trabajo el sábado, pero gano mucho dinero.
>
> Ana

Fill in the spaces. Choose the correct words from the box.

fun	good	clothes	souvenirs	poor
not bad	food	hours	Ana	strict

Example: It's an email from ......Ana...................... .

(i) The shop sells ....

(ii) Ana doesn't like the ....

(iii) The manager is ....

(iv) The pay is ....

> Use common sense when filling in gaps – many of the answers can only be used in one or two circumstances.

(Total for Question 28 = 4 marks)

Holiday jobs

F

29 Listen to some parents discussing their children's jobs. Where do they work?
Listen and put a cross in the correct box.

	A supermarket	B office	C home	D hotel	E café	F garage
Example: Julián			X			
(i) María						
(ii) Antonio						
(iii) David						
(iv) Carolina						

(Total for Question 29 = 4 marks)

My work experience

Where did you work?

E

30 Where did they do their work experience?

Simón
Trabajé en una farmacia.

Catalina
Hice mis prácticas como camarera.

Fernando
Pasé la semana ayudando a mis profesores.

Manu
Hice mis prácticas como recepcionista en el hotel Miramar.

Alicia
Básicamente trabajé como dependienta.

Put a cross in the appropriate box.

	Simón	Catalina	Fernando	Alicia	Manu
Example: worked in a pharmacy	X				
(i) worked in a shop					
(ii) worked in a restaurant					
(iii) worked in a hotel					
(iv) worked in a school					

(Total for Question 30 = 4 marks)

Susana's work experience

D

31 Susana is talking about her work experience. What does she mention? Put a cross in the **four** correct boxes.

Example: her place of work	X
A her colleagues	
B her journey to work	
C her lunch time activities	
D disadvantages of the job	
E the clothes she wore	
F the money she earned	
G the days she worked	
H the work she wants to do in the future	

(Total for Question 31 = 4 marks)

Work experience

Work experience

Ⓒ

32 Read the comments below. Is the opinion positive or negative? Put a cross in the correct box.

	Work	Opinion	Positive 😊	Negative 😣
Example:	fontanero	Mi trabajo era interesante.	X	
(i)	mecánico	Las horas de trabajo se hacían demasiado largas.		
(ii)	dependiente	Algunos de los clientes eran bastante antipáticos.		
(iii)	camarero	Este trabajo cansaba mucho.		
(iv)	jardinero	Me gustaba estar al aire libre.		

(Total for Question 32 = 4 marks)

> It isn't always obvious if the speaker is positive or negative, especially if they don't use phrases such as *me gusta*, so make sure you revise words such as *bastante* (quite), and *demasiado* (too).

Carmen's work experience

33 Listen to Carmen talking about her work experience. What does she mention?
Listen and put a cross in the **four** appropriate boxes.

Example: where she worked	X
A the other employees	
B her journey to work	
C how long she worked	
D disadvantages of this kind of work	
E her ambitions	
F what the best aspects were	
G the days she worked	
H what she wants to do in the future	

(Total for Question 33 = 4 marks)

Dialogues and messages

School telephone message

Part A

34 Listen to the message. Put a cross in the correct box to complete each sentence.

Example: San Bernardo school is ...

A unique.	B specialist.	C certified.
	X	

(i) The school is ...

A safe.	B large.	C ambitious.

(ii) It has the latest ...

A technology.	B courses.	C resources.

(iii) The teachers have the highest ...

A salaries.	B expectations.	C qualifications.

(iv) You can find out more information ...

A on the website.	B in a leaflet.	C at the help desk.

(Total for Question 34A = 4 marks)

Part B

Listen to the second message. Put a cross in the **four** correct boxes.

Example: This is a school number.	X
A You have to speak to the operator.	
B You can report a pupil absent by pressing number 1.	
C To speak to reception you have to press number 3.	
D You can leave a message.	
E You will have to call back.	
F You have to leave your contact details.	
G Someone will get back to you.	

(Total for Question 34B = 4 marks)

Language of the internet

 Internet

E **35** Read the following article.

> ## ¡Abuela a tope con Internet!
>
> Cada tarde la abuelita doña Ángeles se mete en la web. Recibe correos electrónicos de todas partes del mundo. Pasa unas cuatro horas en el ordenador. Ángeles escribe en español, pero está aprendiendo inglés y le ayudan sus nuevos amigos de Estados Unidos. Su marido no es tan hábil con la tecnología. Dice que es demasiado complicada.

Answer the following questions **in English.**

(a) When does Ángeles use the computer?

.... **(1 mark)**

(b) How long does she spend on line?

.... **(1 mark)**

(c) What are her American e-friends teaching her?

.... **(1 mark)**

(d) Why doesn't her husband use the internet?

.... **(1 mark)**

(Total for Question 35 = 4 marks)

> Technology vocabulary can appear in many topics, so make sure you have learned relevant words.

 Technology

C **36** Listen to Ana and Daniel talking about technology. How do they use it? Put a cross in the **four** correct boxes.

	Ana	Daniel
Example: e-mail	X	
(i) texting		
(ii) looking for work		
(iii) sharing photos		
(iv) surfing		
(v) downloading music		

(Total for Question 36 = 4 marks)

79

Internet pros and cons

Internet dangers

37 Read this article.

Nuestro profesor invitó al colegio a una experta en informática para aconsejarnos sobre la seguridad en Internet. Todos tuvimos la oportunidad de trabajar con ella repasando nuestros blogs y considerando su contenido.

Me di cuenta inmediatamente de que había incluido en los míos mucha información personal que comprometía mi privacidad y que me exponía al peligro. También me explicó que había cometido un grave error al enseñar el escudo del cole en mi blog sobre los deberes. Así cualquiera podría localizarme a través del cole y de la ciudad. Para alguien con malas intenciones, sería fácil buscar nuestro escudo en Internet. Esa persona podría entonces encontrar mi barrio, y a mí.

Otras pistas personales que dejé incluyen el nombre y la dirección del parque que frecuento cada día para quedar con mis amigos. Ahora entiendo cómo eso podría ayudar a alguien a localizarme.

La última y mayor equivocación fue poner una foto reciente mía que muestra claramente mi edad. Ahora tengo mucho más cuidado. He mirado y he cambiado mucha información en mi página web y escribo con más precaución cuando hablo en línea.

Esme

Answer the questions **in English**.

(a) Why was an expert invited to the school?

.... (1 mark)

(b) What did the expert help the students do?

.... (1 mark)

(c) Why was Esme at risk ?

.... (1 mark)

(d) What mistake did Esme make when writing about homework ?

.... (1 mark)

(e) How could someone identify Esme's address? Give **two** details.

....

.... (2 marks)

(f) How has Esme's attitude changed ? Give **two** details.

....

.... (2 marks)

(Total for Question = 8 marks)

Nouns and articles

Remember not all words ending in *a* are feminine or ending in *o* are masculine! There are exceptions.

1   Write the correct definite article *el, la, los, las*.

Example: ......la........ gente

1	.... mesa	6	.... piso
2	.... fútbol	7	.... ciencias
3	.... patatas fritas	8	.... guisantes
4	.... dientes	9	.... problema
5	.... mano	10	.... foto

2   Complete the sentence with either the definite article *el, la, los, las* or the indefinite article *un, una*. Remember to think about gender and whether it is singular or plural.

Example: En casa tengo .....un....... perro que es negro y blanco.

  1   En mi opinión, las zanahorias son más ricas que .... judías verdes.

  2   En mi casa hay .... cuarto de baño y tres dormitorios.

  3   No me gusta nada .... francés porque es complicado.

  4   Todos .... martes tengo club de ajedrez.

  5   En mi estuche hay .... regla y tres bolígrafos.

  6   Mi instituto es grande y hay .... salón de actos.

  7   Me he torcido .... tobillo y me duele mucho.

  8   .... domingo fuimos a una piscina al aire libre cerca de mi casa.

Often we use articles in English when in Spanish they are not needed, e.g. talking about jobs, after *sin* and *con*, and after the verb *hablar*.

Sometimes we use articles in Spanish when we would not in English, e.g. talking generally (noun at the start of a sentence), expressing opinions, before the days of the week (*el lunes voy a …*).

3   Read the sentences and cross out any articles that have been used where they are not needed.

Example: No tengo ~~un~~ coche porque prefiero viajar en metro.

  1   Vivo en un cómodo bloque de pisos en las afueras.

  2   Mi padre es un dentista y mi madre es una enfermera.

  3   Hablo el español y el sueco.

  4   Escribo con un lápiz en mi clase de matemáticas.

  5   El sábado voy a la casa de mis abuelos.

  6   El deporte es muy importante para llevar una vida sana.

  7   Odio el dibujo porque no puedo dibujar bien.

  8   Se puede reservar dos habitaciones con una ducha.

Adjectives

Most adjectives agree as follows:	end in *–o*: *alto* / *alta* / *altos* / *altas*
end in *–e*: add *–s* in the plural	end in **consonant***: add *–es* in the plural
*Nationalities also have a separate feminine singular form: *españo**la***	

1 Find the correct adjective from the list. Remember that as well as making sense, the adjective must agree with the noun.

Example: una abogada .....seria...............

1 una casa ....

2 dos gatos ....

3 un vestido ....

4 las películas son ....

5 el profesor es ....

6 las actrices son ....

7 la playa es ....

8 nuestros coches son ....

adosada
baratos
español
interesantes
preciosa
rojo
seria
simpáticas
traviesos

2 Choose the correct adjective.

Example: Vivo en un apartamento muy *pequeña* / *pequeño* / *pequeños*.

1 Me alojé en un hotel *lujoso* / *lujosa* / *lujosos* de cuatro estrellas.

2 Me gusta llevar pantalones *cómodas* / *cómodos* / *cómodo*.

3 Creo que mi instituto es bastante *bueno* / *buen* / *buena*.

4 El paisaje era *impresionantes* / *impresionante* / *impresionanto*.

5 La estación de tren está siempre *limpia* / *limpio* / *limpias*.

6 Me encantan las ciencias porque son muy *útiles* / *útil* / *útilas*.

Some adjectives have shortened forms which are positioned before the noun:
un coche bueno ⟶ un buen coche

3 Write out these sentences with the correct adjective in the correct place.

Example:

Suelo comer fruta porque es sana y deliciosa. (mucho / mucha)

Suelo comer .....mucha.............. fruta porque es sana y deliciosa.

1 En Inglaterra hay gente que habla muy bien griego. (poco / poca)

....

2 Lo mejor es que tiene un jardín. (bonito / bonita)

....

3 Estamos porque hace buen tiempo. (contento / contentas)

....

4 En el futuro habrá una estatua aquí en la plaza. (gran / grandes)

....

5 Nuestro apartamento está en el piso. (primera / primer)

....

6 Mis primas son pero viven en Escocia. (alemán / alemanas)

....

Possessives and pronouns

1   Complete the table with the missing possessive adjectives.

English	Spanish singular	Spanish plural
my	mi	
your		tus
his / her / its		
our		nuestros / nuestras
your		
their	su	

2   Complete the phrase with the correct possessive adjective.

1 My house is big.   .... casa es grande.

2 His brother is the oldest.   .... hermano es el mayor.

3 Their sons play tennis.   .... hijos juegan al tenis.

4 My favourite films are comedies.   .... películas preferidas son las comedias.

5 Its food is healthy.   .... comida es sana.

Possessive pronouns are like possessive adjectives but replace the noun they describe.
They must agree with the noun they replace!

In Spanish they are always accompanied by the definite article:

el mío / la mía, los míos / las mías = mine	el tuyo / la tuya = yours
el suyo / la suya = his/hers	el nuestro / la nuestra = ours

---

3   Complete these comparisons with the correct possessive pronoun.

Example: Nuestras toallas son más pequeñas que ..... las tuyas .... (yours)
           (Our towels are smaller than yours.)

1 Tu perro es más feroz que .... (mine)

2 Mis gafas son menos feas que .... (his)

3 Tu profe de historia es más callado que .... (ours)

4 Su abrigo es más cómodo que .... (yours)

4   Rewrite the phrases to create one sentence using the relative pronoun *que*.

Example: Tengo un hermano. Se llama Diego ⟶ ..... Tengo un hermano que se llama Diego. ....

1 María tiene un gato. Es negro y pequeño.

    ....

2 Vivimos en un pueblo. Está en el norte de Inglaterra.

    ....

3 En la clase de literatura tengo que leer un libro. Es muy aburrido.

    ....

Comparisons

To form the comparative:	*más* + adjective + *que* = more … than
	menos + adjective + *que* = less … than
	tan + adjective + *como* = as … as

1   Read the English and then complete the Spanish sentence with the correct comparative adjectives.

Example: My sister is taller than my brother.

Mi hermana es ..... *más alta que* .... mi hermano.

1   My mother is thinner than my father.

Mi madre es .... mi padre.

2   Mariela is less patient than Francisco.

Mariela es .... Francisco.

3   This bus is slower than the train.

Este autobús es .... el tren.

4   Fruit is as healthy as vegetables.

La fruta es .... las verduras.

5   This shirt is as expensive as that jacket.

Esta camisa es .... aquella chaqueta.

Remember!

el / la mejor, los / las mejores = the best

el / la peor, los / las peores = the worst

---

2   Write out the correct superlative sentence.

Example: Esta cafetería es ..... *la menos cara* .... (the least expensive)

1   Mi profesor de inglés es .... (the best)

2   Mis deberes de religión son .... (the worst)

3   Mi mejor amiga es .... de la clase. (the smallest)

4   Sus perros son .... (the most intelligent)

5   Las noticias de Telecinco son .... (the least boring)

| *el / la* | | *más* | | | = the most |
| *los / las* | + | *menos* | + | adjective | = the least |

---

3   Translate these sentences into Spanish.

To translate words like 'incredibly' or 'extremely' don't forget to use the ending *ísimo/a*.

1   My car is the cheapest. ...... *Mi coche es el más barato* ....

2   My cousin is lazier than your uncle. ....

3   Her mobile phone is incredibly small. ....

4   The Spanish exam is extremely easy. ....

5   Horror films are as exciting as action films. ....

6   My school is the ugliest! ....

7   Science is less boring than geography. ....

8   Messi is the best. ....

Other adjectives

Demonstrative adjectives are used to indicate which thing/person you are referring to ('this', 'those', etc.). There are three in Spanish: one for 'this'/'these', and two for 'that'/'those' (to distinguish between 'that' and 'that further away'). All forms need to agree in number and gender.

1 Complete the table with the correct demonstrative adjective in the box below.

Masculine singular	Feminine singular	Masculine plural	Feminine plural	Meaning
este				this / these
	esa			that / those
		aquellos		that (over there) / those (over there)

2 Translate into Spanish. (o/t = 'over there')

    1 these boots ....

    2 this t-shirt ....

    3 that girl (o/t) ....

    4 those bananas ....

    5 that mobile phone ....

    6 those magazines (o/t) ....

    7 this iPod ....

    8 that film ....

    9 that train (o/t) ....

    10 these hats ....

    11 those strawberries ....

    12 those boys (o/t) ....

3 Complete the sentence with the correct indefinite adjective in the box below.

cada	todo / toda	algún / alguna
mismo / misma	todos / todas	algunos / algunas
mismos / mismas		

    1 Juega al baloncesto .... (every) día.

    2 Siempre da la .... (same) opinión.

    3 Conozco a .... (some) chicas que trabajan como peluqueras.

    4 Ayer, ... (all) los alumnos hicieron sus exámenes.

    5 Mi amigo tiene el .... (same) ordenador portátil que yo.

4 Fill in the gaps in the text using both demonstrative and indefinite adjectives. The text is translated for you below.

El año pasado fui de vacaciones con mi familia. **1** .... los años vamos al sur de Inglaterra, pero este año fuimos a España. **2** .... de mis amigos han ido a España, pero ésta fue mi primera vez. ¡Me gustó mucho! **3** .... los españoles que conocimos eran muy amables y **4** .... hablaban muy bien inglés. En España, a los jóvenes les gusta la **5** .... ropa que a los jóvenes ingleses y nos divierten los **6** .... pasatiempos. ¡Fue muy interesante!

Last year I went on holiday with my family. Every year we go to the South of England but this year we went to Spain. Some of my friends have been to Spain but this was my first time. I liked it a lot! All the Spanish people we met were really nice and some spoke very good English. In Spain, the young people love the same clothes as English young people and we like the same hobbies. It was really interesting!

Pronouns

1 Complete the table with the correct pronouns in English or Spanish.

yo	
	you singular
	he
ella	

	we (masc.)
nosotras	
vosotros	
	you plural (fem.)
ellos	
	they (fem.)

A pronoun replaces a noun. An object pronoun has the action (shown by the verb) done to it. It can be direct or indirect.

She sent it to me. – **it** = direct object; **me** = indirect object

Direct object pronouns: *me, te, lo/la, nos, os, los/las*

Position of the object pronouns:
- Before a conjugated verb: *lo compro* (I buy it), *lo he comprado* (I have bought it)
- After a negative: *no lo compro* (I don't buy it)
- At the end of an infinitive or gerund (or before the verb): *voy a comprarlo / lo voy a comprar* (I am going to buy it), *estoy comprándolo / lo estoy comprando* (I am buying it)

---

2 Replace the noun with the correct object pronoun.

Example: Miguel ha perdido la maleta. → .....Miguel la ha perdido.............

1 Hemos perdido las llaves. ....

2 Han perdido la moto. ....

3 Teresa come el bocadillo. ....

4 Compro el vestido. ....

5 No bebo limonada. ....

6 No lavo la ropa. ....

7 Quiero escribir un correo electrónico. ....

8 No quiero leer esa novela. ....

9 Necesito la información ahora. ....

10 Vamos a vender la casa. ....

> Remember!
> You only need to replace the noun. The verb will stay the same.

3 Translate these sentences, which use direct and indirect object pronouns, into English or Spanish.

> Indirect object pronouns: **me, te, le, nos, os, les**

Example: Le di mi cuaderno de matemáticas. → .....I gave him my Maths exercise book.......

1 Le voy a llamar esta tarde. ....

2 Les visité ayer. ....

3 Lo haré si tengo tiempo. ....

4 Los vendo en el mercado. ....

5 ¿Les has visto? ....

6 She came to visit me at home. ....

7 They sent me the reservation. ....

8 I am going to buy them online. ....

The present tense

> To form the present tense, replace the infinitive ending with:
>
> –ar verbs: *o, as, a, amos, áis, an*
>
> –er verbs: *o, es, e, emos, éis, en*
>
> –ir verbs: *o, es, e, imos, ís, en*
>
> *Tú* is used for people you know and in the present tense will always end in s.
>
> *Usted* is the formal word for you and takes the same ending as *él* or *ella*, and therefore has no s at the end.

1   Write the verb in the correct person.

     Example: escuchar (tú) → ....*escuchas*........

     1 vivir (nosotros) → ....

     2 bailar (ellas) → ....

     3 vender (yo) → ....

     4 llevar (vosotros) → ....

     5 odiar (tú) → ....

     6 comer (él) → ....

     7 salir (nosotros) → ....

     8 escuchar (usted) → ....

2   Choose the correct verb for each phrase.

     Example: En mi tiempo libre (practico) / *practican* deportes.

     1 Mis padres *comemos* / *comen* mucha carne.

     2 Mi hermana y yo *vive* / *vivimos* en un barrio precioso.

     3 ¿A qué hora *tienes* / *tienen* tu clase de natación?

     4 Nunca *habla* / *hablan* en francés porque son tímidos.

     5 Usted *debes* / *debe* firmar aquí.

     6 Nuestro amigo es paciente y nunca *grita* / *gritáis*.

     7 Normalmente *chateas* / *chateo* con mis amigos por Internet.

     8 A veces su profesor *lee* / *leen* en clase.

     9 ¿Usted qué *piensa* / *pensáis* del precio de la gasolina?

     10 *Puedes* / *Podéis* comprar vuestros billetes aquí.

> In the present tense, *er* and *ir* verbs are only different for the *nosotros* and *vosotros* parts of the verb and so there are fewer endings to learn!

3   Write the correct part of the verb in each sentence. Watch out for stem changing verbs!

     Example: Mis amigos .....*estudian*.................... inglés, francés y español. (estudiar)

     1 Nos gusta la comida italiana y esta noche .... pizza. (cenar)

     2 Los mecánicos a veces .... al aire libre. (trabajar)

     3 Me levanto temprano y .... a las ocho y media. (desayunar)

     4 Limpia su dormitorio y luego .... la mesa. (poner)

     5 Nunca comemos caramelos, pero .... pasteles a menudo. (comprar)

     6 ¿Cuánto .... las cebollas? (costar)

     7 .... un cartón de leche, pero no tengo dinero. (querer)

     8 Los niños .... mucho hoy en día. (pedir)

Reflexives and irregulars

1 Write the correct reflexive pronoun next to each part of the verbs *afeitarse* and *vestirse*.

	afeito			visto
te	afeitas			vistes
	afeita			viste
	afeitamos			vestimos
	afeitáis			vestís
se	afeitan			visten

2 Complete the sentence with the correct reflexive pronoun.

Example: A veces mis amigos no .....se....... lavan.

1 Normalmente, los sábados, ... levanta a las nueve y media.

2 Mis amigos no .... peinan, pero yo me peino siempre.

3 ¿A qué hora .... despiertas los domingos?

4 Los profesores .... quejan mucho de sus alumnos.

5 Mis primos .... llaman John y Emma.

6 .... levantamos temprano para ir de vacaciones.

7 ¿ .... ducháis por la mañana o por la tarde?

8 .... lavas y te vistes antes de ir al colegio.

3 Rewrite the story for Olivia. Change all the verbs in the 'I' form to the 'she' form. Don't forget to change the non-reflexive verbs too!

> Todos los días me levanto temprano para ir a trabajar. Trabajo en una tienda de ropa famosa. Primero me lavo los dientes y luego me ducho y me visto. Bajo las escaleras y desayuno cereales con fruta. Siempre me peino en la cocina. Después, me lavo la cara en el cuarto de baño que está abajo, al lado de la cocina. Me pongo la chaqueta y salgo a las ocho y media porque el autobús llega a las nueve menos cuarto. Vuelvo a casa a las siete de la tarde.

Todos los días Olivia se levanta ....

....

....

....

....

....

....

....

....

> Remember! Some verbs are regular but have an irregular ending in the first person singular. *Poner* is one of those verbs: *pongo, pones, pone*, etc. It can be reflexive when it means putting on clothes. Watch out for *salir*, too – the first person is *salgo*.

Ser and *estar*

> *ser*: use for permanent things (e.g. nationality, occupation, colour, size, personality)
>
> *estar*: use for temporary things (e.g. illness, appearance, feelings) and location

1 Write the correct form of the verb *ser* or *estar*.

Example: ......Somos...... ingleses y vivimos en Londres. (ser – nosotros)

1 ¿Dónde .... el banco? (estar – objeto él / ella)

2 Mis abuelas .... muy generosas. (ser – ellos / ellas)

3 .... de Madrid, pero trabajo en Barcelona. (ser – yo)

4 El vestido .... verde con flores blancas. (ser – objeto)

5 .... las cuatro y media de la tarde. (ser – ellos / ellas)

6 El armario .... enfrente de la puerta. (estar – objeto él / lla)

7 .... muy tristes hoy porque las vacaciones han terminado. (estar – vosotros)

8 .... listos para el examen de teatro. (estar – nosotros)

2 Now translate the sentences from exercise 1 into English. In brackets, write down the reason why the verb is *ser* or *estar*.

Example: We are English and we live in London. ("ser" for nationalities) ....

1 ....

2 ....

3 ....

4 ....

5 ....

6 ....

7 ....

8 ....

3 Tick the phrases which use the correct verb 'to be'. Correct those which are wrong.

Example: Estoy en Francia de vacaciones. ✓

La plaza es a mano izquierda. ✗ La plaza está a mano izquierda. ....

1 Somos británicos y hablamos inglés.

....

2 Mi amigo está inteligente y tiene el pelo negro.

....

3 Me duele la cabeza y soy enfermo.

....

4 Mi perro ha muerto y estoy muy triste.

....

5 Su primo es italiano y trabaja como diseñador.

....

6 Mi madre está dependienta y mi padre está ingeniero.

....

7 Creo que hoy, después de ir a la peluquería, estoy guapa.

....

8 Mi casa está bastante pequeña, tiene solo un dormitorio.

....

The gerund

> Gerunds are –ing words (playing, singing, etc.). To form them replace the infinitive endings as follows: *hablar – hablando, comer – comiendo, vivir – viviendo*.
>
> Remember! Some verbs have irregular gerunds:
>
> *caer* ⟶ *cayendo*   *oír* ⟶ *oyendo*   *poder* ⟶ *pudiendo*
>
> Some stem-changing *ir* verbs also change their stem in the gerund:
>
> *pedir* ⟶ *pidiendo*   *dormir* ⟶ *durmiendo*

1   Change the following infinitives into the gerund, and write their meanings in English.

    Example: beber ⟶ .....*bebiendo - drinking*.............

    1 comer ⟶ ....   **6** asistir ⟶ ....

    2 saltar ⟶ ....   **7** escribir ⟶ ....

    3 correr ⟶ ....   **8** escuchar ⟶ ....

    4 tomar ⟶ ....   **9** aprender ⟶ ....

    5 dormir ⟶ ....   **10** poder ⟶ ....

2   What are these people doing? Write sentences using the words from the box.

comer pizza	nadar en la piscina	tocar la guitarra
hablar con amigos	escuchar música	ver una película
navegar por Internet	escribir una postal	montar en bicicleta

    Example: (he) .....*Está nadando en la piscina.*...............................

    1 (she) ....   **4** (we) ....
       ....

    2 (I) ....   **5** (you) ....
       ....

    3 (they) ....
       ....

> The imperfect continuous is formed using the imperfect tense of *estar* + the gerund:
>
> *estaba comiendo* – I was eating
>
> *estar* in the imperfect tense: *estaba, estabas, estaba, estábamos, estabais, estaban*

3   Translate the first part of the missing sentences into Spanish.

    Example: (I was fishing) .....*Estaba pescando*........................... cuando me caí al agua.

    1 (he was sailing) .... cuando llegó la tormenta.

    2 (they were eating) .... cuando su madre les llamó.

    3 (we were sunbathing) .... cuando empezó a llover.

    4 (you were singing) .... cuando salió el tren.

    5 (we were watching TV) .... cuando nuestro padre volvió a casa.

    6 (I was playing video games) .... cuando llamó.

    7 (you all were listening to the teacher) .... cuando entró el perro.

    8 (she was swimming in the sea) .... cuando el tiburón apareció.

The preterite tense

The preterite tense is used to describe completed actions in the past. Replace the infinitive ending with:

–ar verbs: *é, aste, ó, amos, asteis, aron*

–er and *–ir* verbs: *í, iste, ió, imos, isteis, ieron*

Remember! There are lots of irregular verbs in the preterite.

Some have irregular spellings in the first person: *saqué, toqué, crucé, empecé, llegué, jugué*
The most common irregular verbs are: *ir, ser, hacer, dar, decir, estar* and *tener*.

1   Write the correct verb in the preterite.

    Example: comer (tú) ➞ ......*comiste*......

    1   sacar (ellos) ➞ ....

    2   volver (nosotros) ➞ ....

    3   comprar (él) ➞ ....

    4   llegar (tú) ➞ ....

    5   trabajar (vosotros) ➞ ....

    6   ir (usted) ➞ ....

    7   dar (yo) ➞ ....

    8   tener (nosotros) ➞ ....

    9   visitar (ellas) ➞ ....

    10   beber (él) ➞ ....

2   Complete the sentences with the correct verb in the preterite. All these sentences use irregular verbs.

    1   La semana pasada .... (ir) a casa de mis amigos.

    2   Mi novio y yo no .... (tener) tiempo para visitar el museo.

    3   Sus padres nos .... (dar) unos regalos bonitos.

    4   Conchita .... (ir) a la playa con su hermano.

    5   Ayer me .... (levantarse) y .... (vestirse) antes de las nueve.

    6   El lunes mis padres .... (hacer) alpinismo en los Pirineos.

    7   "No es verdad", ... (decir) el niño.

    8   El concierto .... (ser) impresionante. Me gustó mucho.

    9   .... (hacer) mis deberes antes de jugar al fútbol.

    10   Anoche .... (tener) que poner y quitar la mesa y luego salí con mis amigos.

3   Read the text in the present tense and rewrite the text, changing all the verbs in bold into the preterite.

    Voy al cine con mis amigos y **vemos** una película de acción. Después **comemos** en un restaurante italiano. **Como** una pizza con jamón y queso, y mi amiga Lola **come** pollo con pasta. **Bebemos** zumo de manzana y mi amigo Tom **come** una torta de chocolate pero yo no **como** postre. Después del restaurante **voy** en tren a casa de mi prima. El viaje **es** largo y aburrido. **Vuelvo** a casa y **me acuesto** a las once de la noche.

    ......*Fui al cine con mis amigos*..

    ....

    ....

    ....

    ....

    ....

    ....

    ....

The imperfect tense

Remember! The imperfect is used:
- to describe repeated actions in the past
- when you would say 'used to' in English
- to describe background details.

Replace the infinitive ending with:

–ar verbs: *aba, abas, aba, ábamos, abais, aban*

–er and *–ir* verbs: *ía, ías, ía, íamos, íais, ían*

1   Tick the sentences which contain imperfect verbs and underline the verbs.

Example: Antes mi colegio ..... *era* .... más pequeño. ✓

1   El miércoles fuimos a la piscina y nadamos durante una hora y media.

2   De pequeños nadábamos en el mar todas las semanas.

3   Había mucha gente en el museo y las estatuas eran preciosas.

4   Mi padre nos preparó una cena vegetariana.

5   Cuando eran más jóvenes, no comían tomate ni lechuga.

6   Gabriela llegó a Madrid en tren para empezar su nuevo trabajo.

7   Ayer nos encontramos en la cafetería y hablamos toda la tarde.

8   Me ponía nervioso cada vez que hacía una prueba de vocabulario.

9   Lo pasé genial porque hizo sol y no llovió.

10   Nevaba todos los días y hacía un frío horrible.

2   Translate the sentences from exercise 1 into English. Explain your choice of tense in brackets.

Example: My school used to be very small. (imperfect for "used to") ....

1   ....

2   ....

3   ....

4   ....

5   ....

6   ....

7   ....

8   ....

9   ....

10   ....

3   Complete the sentences with the correct verb in the past tense. It could be either the preterite or the imperfect.

Example: El sábado .... a la discoteca a bailar y a divertirnos. (ir)

1   Cuando mi hermana ......*fuimos*...... tres años empezó a tocar el piano. (tener)

2   Mi familia .... en el campo, pero ahora tiene un piso en Londres. (vivir)

3   .... lloviendo cuando llegamos al camping. (estar)

4   La semana pasada .... la aspiradora y planché la ropa. (pasar)

5   Todos los días .... en el jardín y plantaban muchas rosas. (trabajar)

6   Hizo compras por Internet y .... mucho dinero. (gastar)

7   Siempre .... fruta y bebíamos mucha agua para estar en forma. (comer)

8   Una vez .... al tenis con mi profesor de inglés, pero no gané. (jugar)

The future tense

> The **near future** tense is used to say what's going to happen. It is formed using the present tense of *ir* + *a* + an infinitive: *Voy a salir a las dos.* I'm going to go out at 2.
>
> Present tense of *ir*: *voy, vas, va, vamos, vais, van*

1   Complete the phrases with the missing parts of the near future tense.

     Example: I am going to buy a dress. Voy .....a........... comprar un vestido.

     1   We are going to play basketball. Vamos a .... al baloncesto.

     2   She is going to lay the table. .... a poner la mesa.

     3   They are going to eat lamb chops. Van .... comer chuletas de cordero.

     4   I am not going to cry. No .... a llorar.

     5   Are you going to watch the film? ¿ .... a ver la película?

     6   You (all) are going to listen and repeat. .... a escuchar y a repetir.

     7   My mother is going to catch the bus. Mi madre .... a coger el autobús.

     8   My friends are going to go to Scotland. Mis amigos van a .... a Escocia.

     9   We are not going to work Saturdays. No .... a trabajar los sábados.

     10   I am going to go out with my girlfriend. .... a salir con mi novia.

> The **future tense** is used to talk about what you will do or what will happen in the future. The future is tense is formed by adding these endings onto the infinitive:
>
> *-é, -ás, -á, -emos, -éis, -án*
>
> Don't forget the accents!
>
> Remember there are some irregular future verbs: *saldré, diré, tendré, haré,* etc.

2   Write the Spanish for these future sentences. Remember to use the future tense when describing what will happen.

     Example: I will buy a dress. ....*Compraré un vestido.*...................

     1   We are going to watch the film. ....

     2   I will not work on Mondays. ....

     3   They are going to catch the underground. ....

     4   He will go to England. ....

     5   They are going to play with my brother. ....

     6   You will go to Spain. ....

3   Complete the text with the correct verbs in the near future tense.

seguir	ser	trabajar	tener	ir	tomarse	ser	vivir	ir

El año que viene mi amiga **1** .... a la universidad a estudiar Biología. Yo no

2 .... a la universidad porque me **3** .... un año sabático. Quiero

trabajar como voluntaria, pero **4** .... que vivir con mis padres para ahorrar

dinero. **5** .... como voluntaria para una asociación benéfica que cuida a los sin

techo. **6** .... muy interesante, pero me imagino que el trabajo

7 .... muy duro también. Mi hermana **8** .... estudiando en el

cole y mi hermano **9** .... en el extranjero.

The conditional

The conditional is used to describe what you would do or what would happen in the future. To form the conditional, you add the following endings to **the infinitive**:

ía, ías, ía, íamos, íais, ían

All verbs use the same endings, but some verbs don't use the infinitive as the stem. These irregular verbs use the same stem as for the future tense.

1 Remember that the conditional is similar to the future tense and adds its endings on to the infinitive. It also has the same irregulars!

Change these future verbs into the conditional. Write the English for each.

Example: haré → haría – I would do

1 compraremos → ....

2 saldrán → ....

3 trabajaréis → ....

4 estará → ....

5 jugarás → ....

6 vendremos → ....

7 podrás → ....

8 habrá → ....

2 In an ideal world what would happen next year? Create sentences using the conditional.

Example: Mi madre compraría un perro.

1 Mi profesor .... de vacaciones.

2 Nuestros primos .... el sol en la playa.

3 El jefe no .... todos los días.

4 Mis amigos y yo .... la lotería.

5 No .... contaminación atmosférica.

6 Más gente .... el transporte público.

7 Las empresas no .... el agua.

8 Los gobiernos .... contra la pobreza mundial.

9 Mi equipo de fútbol .... la liga nacional.

10 Mi hermano y yo no .... el dormitorio.

malgastar
(= to squander)
ir
ganar
haber
compartir
comprar
trabajar
usar
luchar
tomar
ganar

3 Give advice using the conditional of *deber* or *poder* to help these people.

Example: Tengo dolor de cabeza. -

Deberías/Podrías tomar estas pastillas.

1 No puedo dormir.

....

2 Como demasiado chocolate.

....

3 No tengo energía.

....

tomar estas pastillas
acostarte temprano
comer más fruta y verduras
comprar ropa de segunda mano
consumir menos energía
ir al médico
ir al dentista
hacer más ejercicio
evitar el estrés

4 Estoy enfermo. ....

5 Estoy cansado todo el tiempo. ....

6 Me duelen las muelas. ....

7 Quiero reducir la contaminación. ....

8 Debo gastar menos dinero. ....

The perfect and pluperfect tenses

The perfect tense is used to talk about what someone **has done** or what **has happened**; the pluperfect about what someone **had done** or what **had happened**.

Perfect: present tense of *haber* + a past participle.

Pluperfect: imperfect tense of *haber* + a past participle.

To form the past participle replace the infinitive ending with:
–ar verbs: **ado**
–er and *–ir* verbs: **ido**

1   Complete the table with the correct parts of the verb *haber*.

	Perfect tense (I have … etc.)	Pluperfect tense (I had … etc.)	+ past participles (spoken, eaten, lived, etc.)
yo	he		
tú			
él / ella / usted		había	hablado comido vivido
nosotros / nosotras	hemos		
vosotros / vosotras			
ellos / ellas / ustedes		habían	

2   Translate these phrases into English or Spanish. The box below will help you.

Example: He hablado con él. ......I have spoken to him..

   1   Hemos perdido el coche. ....
   2   ¿Has estudiado español? ....
   3   Han comprado un ordenador portátil. ....
   4   He hecho mis deberes. ....
   5   Hemos visto un documental muy informativo. ....
   6   I have broken my arm. ....
   7   They have lost their suitcase. ....
   8   We have eaten lots of sweets. ....
   9   Have you visited the museum today? ....
   10   The shop assistant has opened the shop. ....

Irregular past participles!

abrir → abierto	escribir → escrito	poner → puesto	ver → visto
decir → dicho	hacer → hecho	romper → roto	volver → vuelto

3   Change the verbs into the pluperfect to tell the story.

Esta mañana ha sido horrible. 1 ......Había desayunado.......... (desayunar) cuando sonó mi móvil. Mi amiga 2 .... (perder) la bolsa en el polideportivo y no tenía dinero suficiente para pagar la entrada. Ella 3 .... (nadar) en la piscina y también 4 .... (hacer) una clase de aerobic. Así que fui al polideportivo para ayudar a mi amiga, pero yo me 5 .... (dejar) la bici en el cole y por eso cogí el autobús. El viaje duró mucho y cuando llegué, mi amiga ya 6 .... (encontrar) su bolsa y su dinero. ¡Qué desastre!

Giving instructions

To give commands:

– to one person (*tú*): use the 'you' singular form of the present tense, minus the final *s*:
¡Escucha! Listen!   *¡Abre!* Open!

– to more than one person (*vosotros*): change the final *r* of the infinitive to *d*:
¡Escuchad! Listen!   *¡Abrid!* Open!

Irregular *tú* / *vosotros* commands include:

	decir	hacer	ir	oír	poner	salir	tener	venir
English	say	make/do	go	hear	put	leave	have	come
tú	di	haz	ve	oye	pon	sal	ten	ven
vosotros	decid	haced	id	oíd	poned	salid	tened	venid

1 Change the following infinitives into familiar singular commands (*tú*). Be careful, some are irregular in command form.

Example: Hablar más → .....Habla más.......

1 Doblar a la derecha → ....
2 Cruzar la plaza → ....
3 Pasar el puente → ....
4 Tener cuidado → ....
5 Venir aquí → ....

6 Cantar más bajo → ....
7 Leer en voz alta → ....
8 Escuchar bien → ....
9 Poner la mesa → ....
10 Hacer este ejercicio → ....

2 Now change the above commands into familiar plural ones (*vosotros*). Remember, to form the *vosotros* commands, you change the *r* of the infinitive to *d*.

Example: Habla más. → .....Hablad más..........

1 ....
2 ....
3 ....
4 ....
5 ....

6 ....
7 ....
8 ....
9 ....
10 ....

3 Translate these sentences into Spanish, using either *tú* or *vosotros* commands.

Example: Listen now! (vosotros) → .....¡Escuchad ahora!.......

1 Download the music! (tú) ....
2 Turn left! (vosotros) ....
3 Clear the table! (tú) ....
4 Make the bed! (tú) ....
5 Do the hovering! (vosotros) ....

The present subjunctive

The subjunctive is used in a range of contexts, e.g.

– to express doubt or uncertainty: *No creo que venga.* I don't think he's coming.

– to express a wish with **querer que**: *Quiero que te calles.* I wish you'd be quiet.

– after **cuando** with the future: *Cuando llegue, le contestaré.* When he arrives, I'll ask him.

– after **ojalá**: *Ojalá haga sol.* Let's hope it's sunny.

– to express a negative opinion: *No es verdad que sea tímida.* It's not true that she's shy.

– to give negative *tú* commands.

The subjunctive is formed by replacing the *–o* ending of the present tense 'I' form with:

–ar verbs: *e, es, e, emos, éis, en*

–er and *–ir* verbs: *a, as, a, amos, áis, an*

Therefore verbs which are irregular in the first person in the present are irregular in the present subjunctive.

ir and *ser* have irregular stems: *vay– (ir)* and *se– (ser)*. The endings are the same.

1   Change these verbs from the present indicative into the present subjunctive.

   Example: tenemos → ......*tengamos*.........

   1 habla → ....   6 sale → ....

   2 comen → ....   7 puede → ....

   3 voy → ....   8 hacen → ....

   4 vives → ....   9 encuentro → ....

   5 trabajáis → ....   10 somos → ....

2   Use the present subjunctive to make these positive *tú* commands into negative ones.

   Example: Habla con él. → .....*No hables con él.*..

   1 Come este pastel. → ....

   2 Compra aquel vestido.→ ....

   3 Toma estas pastillas. → ....

   4 Bebe un vaso de zumo de naranja. → ....

   5 Ve esta película romántica. → ....

   6 Firma aquí. → ....

   7 Rellena el formulario. → ....

   8 Salta tres veces. → ....

3   Complete these sentences with the correct verb in the present subjunctive.

   Example: Ojalá mi amiga .....*venga*.............. (venir) a visitarme.

   1 No creo que los jóvenes .... (trabajar) tanto.

   2 No es cierto que .... (hacer) buen tiempo el fin de semana.

   3 Ojalá nosotros .... (tener) suerte con los exámenes.

   4 No creo que mis profesores .... (ser) estrictos.

   5 Cuando .... (ir) a España, compraré un sombrero.

   6 Dudo que los adolescentes .... (comprar) CD.

Negatives

> To make a sentence negative, use *no* in front of the whole verb:
>
> *No me gusta la música jazz.*   I don't like jazz music.
> *No vamos a visitar el palacio.*   We are not going to visit the palace.

1   Write these sentences in the negative.

    Example: Tengo clase hoy a las diez. → ....*No tengo clase hoy a las diez.*.............

     1   Estudio geografía. → ....

     2   Vamos a las afueras. → ....

     3   Ricardo compró una moto nueva. → ....

     4   Sus padres vieron la tele. → ....

     5   Voy a ir a Francia la semana que viene. → ....

2   Match the English and Spanish.

     1   no … ni … ni …   **a**   never

     2   no … nada   **b**   not … either

     3   no … tampoco   **c**   no/not any

     4   no … nadie   **d**   nothing/not anything

     5   no … jamás   **e**   not … (either) … or …

     6   no … nunca   **f**   never

     7   no … ningún/ninguna   **g**   no one

3   Rewrite the sentence with the negative words.

    Example: Mateo habla mucho de sus vacaciones. (no, nunca)

        ....*Mateo no habla nunca de sus vacaciones.*...

> Note that *ninguno* must agree with the noun it precedes: *ninguna ropa* (no clothes)

     1   Mis profesores enseñan cómo teclear. (no, nunca) ....

     2   En mi casa tuvimos una sala de juegos. (no, jamás) ....

     3   Me he quemado los brazos. (no, nunca) ....

     4   Aquí tengo vestidos, faldas y camisetas. (no, ni, ni, ni) ....

     5   Vas a comprar un coche. (no, ningún) ....

     6   Mis padres escuchan. (no, a nadie) ....

3   Translate the sentences into Spanish. Be careful with the word order.

    Example: He never plays football when it rains.

        ....*Nunca juega al fútbol cuando llueve. / No juega nunca al fútbol cuando llueve.*.....

     1   In the afternoon we never drink coffee. ....

     2   I don't iron, cook or clean. ....

     3   They do not speak any languages. ....

     4   We can't talk to anybody during the exam. ....

        ....

     5   I will never smoke because it is a waste of time. ....

        ....

Special verbs

> A few verbs like *gustar* are generally used in the 3rd person with a pronoun:
> *Me gusta bailar.* I like dancing.
>
> If the thing that is liked is plural, you use ***me gustan***: *Me gustan los perros.* I like dogs.
> *encantar, doler, apetecer* and *hacer falta* behave in the same way:
> *Le duele la garganta.* His throat hurts.
> *Hacer faltan dos vasos.* Two glasses are missing.

1 Complete the table with the correct pronouns.

me	gusta (sing) gustan (plu)	I like
		you like
		he / she / it likes

	gusta (sing) gustan (plu)	we like
		you (all) like
		they like

2 Tick the sentences which use the impersonal verb correctly. Correct the other sentences.

> **Remember!** If the impersonal verb is followed by an infinitive, the singular form is always used:
> *Les **gusta** tocar la guitarra.* = They like to play the guitar.
> You need to use *a* with a proper name: *A Paz le gusta correr.* Paz likes to run.

Example: Me gusta mucho los idiomas y por eso quiero viajar más. ✗

·····Me gustan mucho los idiomas y por eso quiero viajar más.·····

1 A Pilar y a Pablo les interesan los ordenadores y la informática.

....

2 Nos apetecen ir al teatro mañana.

....

3 Es verdad que le duelen mucho las muelas.

....

4 No nos gustan la contaminación atmosférica.

....

5 ¿Te hace falta unas toallas?

....

3 Unjumble the words to make sentences using an impersonal verb.

Example: gustan / las / me / zanahorias / mucho ·····Me gustan mucho las zanahorias.·········

1 falta / abrigo / nos / un / hace ....

2 os / caballos / encantan / los / negros ....

3 María / le / aquellos / zapatos / a / gustan ....

4 quedan / veinte / te / euros / regalo / comprar / para / el

....

5 todo / me / el / la / garganta / tiempo / duele

....

6 encantan / rascacielos / porque / les / son / modernos / los

....

Por and *para*

> Remember that *por* and *para* don't just mean 'for'. They can be translated in various ways depending on the sentence. For example: in, in order to, per, instead of, etc.

1 Translate these sentences, which use *para*, into English.

1 Para mi cumpleaños quiero un móvil nuevo.

....

2 Mi amiga trabaja para un abogado.

....

3 Las aplicaciones para iPhone son increíbles.

....

4 Como muchas verduras y pescado para estar en forma.

....

5 Necesitas la llave para entrar en casa.

....

6 Fumar es muy malo para la salud.

....

7 Van a organizar una fiesta para celebrar el fin de curso.

....

8 Para mí, los deportes son siempre divertidos.

....

2 Rewrite the sentences with the word *por* in the correct place.

Example: Muchas gracias los pantalones. .....Muchas gracias por los pantalones.....

1 El coche rojo pasó las calles antiguas.

....

2 Normalmente la mañana me gusta desayunar cereales y fruta.

....

3 Mandé la reserva correo electrónico.

....

4 Me gustaría cambiar este jersey otro.

....

5 En la tienda ganamos diez euros hora.

....

6 Había mucha basura todas partes.

....

3 Complete the sentence with either *por* or *para*.

Example: .... la tarde prefiero descansar.

1 ....Por........ perder peso, lo más importante es beber mucha agua.

2 Mis amigas compraron unas flores .... la profesora.

3 Tengo que cambiar este diccionario .... otro.

4 Hemos reservado una habitación .... tres noches.

5 Los alumnos tienen que completar los ejercicios .... el lunes.

Questions and exclamations

Don't forget that Spanish question words have accents. Questions and exclamations have an inverted question mark (¿) or exclamation mark (¡) at the beginning.

1 Use the question words in the box to complete the table below.

¿Qué?	¿Cuánto?	¿Dónde?	¿Cuándo?	¿Cuáles?
¿Adónde?	¿Por qué?	¿Cuántos?	¿Cómo?	¿Cuál?

1	Why?	
2	What?	¿Qué?
3	When?	
4	How?	
5	Where?	
6	Where to?	
7	Which?	¿Cuál?
8	Which ones?	
9	How much?	
10	How many?	

2 Match the Spanish and the English for these exclamations. Write the correct letters in the grid.

1 ¡Qué lástima!		**A** What a problem!
2 ¡Qué va!		**B** How strange!
3 ¡Qué rollo!		**C** How cool!
4 ¡Qué difícil!		**D** How terrible!
5 ¡Qué problema!		**E** No way!
6 ¡Qué guay!		**F** What a shame!
7 ¡Qué bien!		**G** How boring!
8 ¡Qué raro!		**H** How embarrassing!
9 ¡Qué vergüenza!		**I** How good!
10 ¡Qué horror!		**J** How difficult!

1	2	3	4	5	6	7	8	9	10
F									

3 Complete the question or exclamation with the appropriate word or phrase.

rollo	guay	por qué	cuánto	dónde	horror

Example: ¿De .....dónde..... son ustedes?

1 Me he roto la pierna. ¡Qué ....!

2 ¿ .... cuesta el jamón serrano?

3 ¿ .... es tu casa, Ramona?

4 Vamos a ir de vacaciones. ¡Qu

...................!

5 El viaje en autocar va a durar ocho horas.

¡Qué ....!

101

Connectives and adverbs

Not all adverbs end in *–mente*:
bien – well   *siempre* – always   *bastante* – enough   *poco* – a little
mal – badly   *demasiado* – too   *a menudo* – frequently / often

1 Turn these adjectives into adverbs. Remember to make them feminine first!

Example: fácil ⟶ ....*fácilmente*...................

1 rápido ⟶ ....
2 difícil ⟶ ....
3 lento ⟶ ....

4 alegre ⟶ ....
5 tranquilo ⟶ ....

2 Match the connectives correctly. Write the correct letter.

1 además de	**A** but
2 y / e	**B** therefore
3 pero	**C** even if
4 sin embargo	**D** also
5 también	**E** and
6 por eso / por lo tanto	**F** if
7 porque	**G** because
8 ya que	**H** then
9 si	**I** or
10 o / u	**J** since
11 aunque	**K** however
12 entonces	**L** as well as

1	2	3	4	5	6	7	8	9	10	11	12
L											

3 Rewrite 1 – 5 with the correct adverb. Complete 6 – 8 with the correct connective.

Example: Los alumnos juegan al rugby. (well) ....*Los alumnos juegan bien al rugby*.................

1 Sus padres cantan en la iglesia. (badly)

   ....

2 No hablo porque soy tímido. (much)

   ....

3 El tren pasa por el túnel. (quickly)

   ....

4 Los pendientes son caros. (too)

   ....

5 Comemos huevos por la mañana. (frequently)

   ....

6 Vamos a ir a la piscina .... hace buen tiempo.

7 Odio mi instituto .... hay acoso escolar.

8 El piso es muy moderno, ... no tiene lavaplatos.

Remember! Adverbs can go before or after the verb they relate to:
Siempre como carne. / Como siempre carne.

Numbers

1 Write the number.

Example: trece ......13..........

A veinte ....

B cuarenta y ocho ....

C nueve ....

D cien ....

E catorce ....

F mil ....

G trescientos ....

H cincuenta y siete ....

I veintitrés ....

J quince ....

K diecinueve ....

L quinientos ....

M un millón ....

N novecientos ....

O ochenta y ocho ....

P setenta y seis ....

Q sesenta y siete ....

R diez ....

S cero ....

T veintinueve ....

2 Write these dates and years in Spanish.

Example: 4 May .... el cuatro de mayo ....

1 1999 ....

2 10 October ....

3 1 January ....

4 3 March ....

5 2013 ....

6 16 November ....

7 30 May ....

8 1968 ....

9 2002 ....

10 21 April ....

Ordinal numbers (*primero, segundo, tercero,* etc.) are not used for dates, except for *primero* which can be used. Both of these are correct:
el uno de diciembre
el primero de diciembre

3 Write down these prices in words.

Example: 48,50 € ..... *cuarenta y ocho euros con cincuenta* ....

1 20,25 € ....

2 59,10 € ....

3 100,75 € ....

4 87 € ....

5 45,20 € ....

6 7,99 € ....

7 86,70 € ....

8 30,65 € ....

Practice Exam Paper: Reading

Edexcel publishes official Sample Assessment Material on its website. This Practice Exam Paper has been written to help you practise what you have learned and may not be representative of a real exam paper.

On the road

1 Read the signs.

A	B	C	D	E	F
Aeropuerto	Metro	Estación de tren	Autopista	Puerto	Parada de autobús

Find the right sign for each statement below. Write the correct letter in each box.

Example: Bus 20 goes to town.	F
(i)	My plane leaves tomorrow.	
(ii)	My train is at 9.	
(iii)	I'm going by car.	
(iv)	My ferry leaves tonight.	

(Total for Question 1 = 4 marks)

In town

2 Where do they want to go?

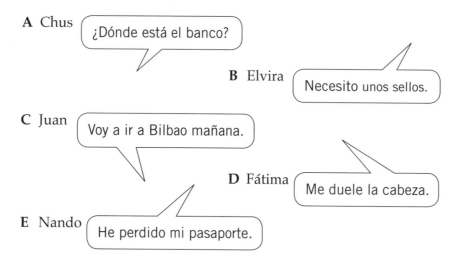

A Chus — ¿Dónde está el banco?

B Elvira — Necesito unos sellos.

C Juan — Voy a ir a Bilbao mañana.

D Fátima — Me duele la cabeza.

E Nando — He perdido mi pasaporte.

Put a cross in the correct box.

	A Chus	B Elvira	C Juan	D Fátima	E Nando
Example: bank	X				
(i) post office					
(ii) chemist					
(iii) station					
(iv) police station					

(Total for Question 2 = 4 marks)

Blogging

3 Read the following blog entries about part-time jobs.

Which places of work
are mentioned?

A office

B home

C shop

D restaurant

E outside

Título: Mi trabajillo

Antonio: Trabajo en una oficina.

Mar: Me encanta trabajar en el restaurante.

Ángel: Trabajo al aire libre con niños.

Isabel: No soporto trabajar en casa.

Martín: Los fines de semana trabajo en una tienda.

Put a cross in the correct box.

	A	**B**	**C**	**D**	**E**	**F**
Example: Antonio	X					
(i) Mar						
(ii) Ángel						
(iii) Isabel						
(iv) Martín						

(Total for Question 3 = 4 marks)

A family holiday

4 Read this e-mail from Juani. What does she say about her holidays in Santander?

¡Hola!

Todos los años mi familia y yo pasamos una semana de vacaciones en la ciudad de Santander. Normalmente nos alojamos en un hotel frente al mar. La playa es bastante bonita, pero para mí, el agua está demasiado fría para nadar.

Muchos turistas vienen a Santander en ferry. La mayoría de los restaurantes tienen buena fama. Muchos turistas quieren comer en uno de los muchos sitios donde sirven pescado y marisco.

A mi madre le gusta comprar recuerdos en las tiendas de la ciudad, mientras que mi padre se entretiene mirando los barcos en el puerto. A mí no me gusta el mercado. Es interesante, pero hay demasiados turistas.

Juani

Put a cross in the **four** correct boxes.

Example: Juani's family visits Isla every year.	X
A The family visit lasts two weeks.	
B The hotel is opposite the sea.	
C Juani enjoys swimming in the sea at Isla beach.	
D The town doesn't receive many British tourists.	
E There are lots of highly rated restaurants in the town.	
F Fish is often available in the restaurants.	
G Juani's mother likes to shop for souvenirs.	
H Juani is very keen on market day in Santander.	

(Total for Question 4 = 4 marks)

Practice Exam Paper: Reading

Sunday trading

B 5 Read this article.

Tiendas abiertas los domingos

Antes cerraban las tiendas los fines de semana, pero ya no. El hecho de que estén abiertas a todas horas atrae mucho a jóvenes y mayores. Preguntamos a algunas personas que estaban de compras cuándo suelen ir a las tiendas.

David (16) nos contó que, simplemente, no tiene tiempo durante la semana para comprar, así que los nuevos horarios le vienen muy bien.

Celia Cruz (85) dice que la compra es su actividad principal. ¡Lo hace a pesar de su edad y le encanta!

El señor López, jefe de un gran complejo comercial cerca de Madrid, nos habló de las ganancias del domingo anterior. Según él, al mediodía el aparcamiento estaba completamente lleno, las cafeterías no tenían sitio suficiente para su clientela y la gente estaba gastando con generosidad. Dijo que la mayoría de los compradores buscaban ropa, sobre todo de moda, aunque también eran populares las tiendas de tecnología y de electrodomésticos. Parece ser que los supermercados ganaron bien, pero menos que el sábado. El señor López está convencido de que las tiendas abiertas veinticuatro horas benefician a los comerciantes y a los consumidores.

What is said about Sunday shopping? Put a cross in the **four** correct boxes.

Example: Shops in the past were closed on Sundays.	X
A Mrs Cruz got to the shops at 1 o'clock.	
B The clothes shops were very busy.	
C David only shops at weekends.	
D Fashion items were popular.	
E Shopping has become the most popular hobby.	
F Sunday opening attracts mainly older shoppers.	
G It wasn't possible to park at midday.	
H The supermarkets sold more on Sunday than on Saturday.	

At A* there may be words you are not familiar with. Read the passage through entirely for gist and then focus on what you do know.

(Total for Question 5 = 4 marks)

Myself and my family

C 6 Read this e-mail from Antonio, then answer the questions on the opposite page.

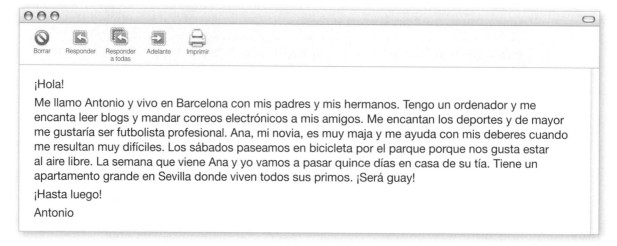

¡Hola!

Me llamo Antonio y vivo en Barcelona con mis padres y mis hermanos. Tengo un ordenador y me encanta leer blogs y mandar correos electrónicos a mis amigos. Me encantan los deportes y de mayor me gustaría ser futbolista profesional. Ana, mi novia, es muy maja y me ayuda con mis deberes cuando me resultan muy difíciles. Los sábados paseamos en bicicleta por el parque porque nos gusta estar al aire libre. La semana que viene Ana y yo vamos a pasar quince días en casa de su tía. Tiene un apartamento grande en Sevilla donde viven todos sus primos. ¡Será guay!

¡Hasta luego!

Antonio

106

Read the email on page 106 and then put a cross next to the **four** things he mentions.

Example: what he uses his computer for	X
A the things to do in his town	
B his free time preferences	
C the food he likes	
D his immediate future plans	
E school work	
F his girlfriend	
G his girlfriend's family	
H his family's house in Seville	

(Total for Question 6 = 4 marks)

Abel Vázquez Cortijo – Paralympian

7 Read this article and put a cross next to the **four** correct statements.

Abel Vázquez empezó a hacer judo influido por sus padres principalmente, ya que ellos también fueron deportistas de éxito en su juventud y representaron a España en equipos nacionales.

Es discapacitado, ya que tiene problemas de visión. Tiene dificultad para leer las letras de tamaño pequeño. También le resulta difícil salir de casa, ya que necesita poner gran atención por donde va caminando.

Todas sus medallas están colocadas en un lugar donde todos puedan verlas, y así comparte su experiencia y motiva a más gente con discapacidades. Dice que lo más importante es la determinación, la responsabilidad y el entusiasmo para realizar nuestros sueños, sean cuales sean tus circunstancias y problemas.

¡Es un buen ejemplo a seguir para todos!

Example: Abel isn't the first successful sportsman in his family.	X
A He can't read or write.	
B He has some difficulty reading.	
C He is blind.	
D He has to be careful when he goes outside.	
E He can't recognise people.	
F He likes to show off his trophies.	
G He has a negative outlook on life.	
H He is a good role model.	

(Total for Question 7 = 4 marks)

Letter to a hotel

8   Read Juan's letter.

Londres, 2 de septiembre de 2012

Hotel Buena Vista

Estimado señor:

El pasado mes de agosto pasé quince días en el hotel Buena Vista con mi familia. Nuestra habitación era muy cómoda y el servicio que ofrecieron los camareros en el restaurante fue excelente. Durante nuestra estancia disfrutamos también de muchas excursiones a muy buen precio.

Quiero darles las gracias por el servicio tan amable. Su hotel es realmente precioso. Intentaremos volver el año que viene.

Atentamente,

Juan López

Put a cross in the correct box.

Example: Juan stayed with ...

A his family.	X
B his friends.	
C his colleagues.	

(i) Juan's visit was ...

A last week.	
B last month.	
C last year.	

(ii) Juan's room was ...

A good size.	
B clean.	
C comfortable.	

(iii) The trips were ...

A cheap.	
B good value.	
C organised.	

(iv) Juan found the service ...

A efficient.	
B effective.	
C friendly.	

(Total for Question 8 = 4 marks)

Problem page

9 Read these problems and responses.

A

Carmen: No sé qué hacer. La gente no para de animarme a hacer cosas que no me apetecen. Tengo miedo a decir que no. ¿Qué puedo hacer?
Respuesta: Carmen, no te desesperes. Simplemente tienes que ser fuerte y lista, y dar excusas creíbles cuando algo no te apetezca. Recuerda que los que son amigos de verdad te van a querer hagas lo que hagas.

B

Gorka: Estoy muy mal porque no tengo dinero para hacer las cosas que quiero. ¿Me puedes aconsejar algo?
Respuesta: Es cuestión de usar tu imaginación, Gorka. Habla con tus amigos para pensar qué cosas podéis hacer por poco dinero.

C

Alba: Estoy muy sola. A pesar de que tengo muchos hermanos, son muy pequeños y donde vivo no tengo amigos de mi edad.
Respuesta: Muy fácil, Alba. Lo mejor es hacerte socia de una organización de tu barrio donde practiquen algún deporte u otra actividad que te guste. Allí harás amigos rápidamente.

D

Ricardo: No sé si me puedes ayudar. Es que estoy muy preocupado porque no sé qué voy a hacer después del colegio. Donde vivo no hay trabajo y no tengo dinero para estudiar en la universidad.
Respuesta: ¡Ante todo no te preocupes! Estudia mucho para sacar buenas notas y haz actividades fuera del colegio. Así tendrás un currículum interesante. El futuro se arreglará solo.

E

Cristiano: ¡Estoy desesperado! Me llevo muy mal con mis padres. Me presionan mucho con los estudios y no me dejan salir con mis amigos. Me tratan como a un niño.
Respuesta: ¡Es imprescindible hablar! Explícales lo que te molesta y escucha sus quejas también. Llega a un acuerdo. Todo es cuestión de equilibrio.

Match the name of the appropriate person with each of the problems listed in the table below. For each problem note the advice given.

Problem	Person	Advice
Example: peer pressure	A	Be your own person.
(i) parents		
(ii) no money		
(iii) worried about the future		
(iv) being lonely		

(Total for Question 9 = 4 marks)

Practice Exam: Listening

Edexcel publishes official Sample Assessment Material on its website. This Practice Exam Paper has been written to help you practise what you have learned and may not be representative of a real exam paper.

Shops

G

1 Listen to these shoppers. What shop do they need to go to?

Put the correct letter in the grid below.

Example:	C
1		2		3		4	

(Total for Question 1 = 4 marks)

Going shopping

F

2 Listen to some young people talking about their shopping. Where do they need to go? Put a cross in the correct box.

	A sweet shop	B florist	C sports shop	D butcher	E bookshop	F chemist
Example:	X					
(i)						
(ii)						
(iii)						
(iv)						

(Total for Question 2 = 4 marks)

My town

E

3 Listen to Javier talking about his town. What does he mention?

A where it is	D the transport system	G the schools
B the size of the town	E the shops	H the type of town
C the activities	F the weather	I the cost of living

Write the letters of the things he mentions in each box.

Example:	A		
(i)		(iii)	
(ii)		(iv)	

(Total for Question 3 = 4 marks)

A trip to the zoo

4 Listen to Conchi, David and Ana talking about their recent trip to the zoo. Who says what? Write the name of the correct person.

Conchi	David	Ana

Example: Who thinks it was a good day out? ......David..............................

1 Who mentions the weather? ....

2 Who mentions the food? ....

3 Who thought the journey was long? ....

4 Who thinks they should go there again? ....

(Total for Question 4 = 4 marks)

Favourite activities

5 Listen to some young people talking about their favourite activities. Which comments do they make?

A I spend my time shopping online.	
B I enjoy reading.	
C I like walking.	
D I like DIY.	
E I like performing arts.	
F I love water sports.	

Write the correct letter in the box.

Example: Jorge	B
(i) Flor	
(ii) Federico	
(iii) Clara	
(iv) Seve	

(Total for Question 5 = 4 marks)

> Use the reading time to think about how you say the activities in Spanish.

Easy reading

6 Listen to Lourdes talking about her latest gadget. Put a cross in the **four** correct boxes.

Example: It is an electronic book.	X
A It is expensive.	
B It can send texts.	
C It is encourages people to read.	
D It is small.	
E It is heavy.	
F You can make the text bigger.	
G You have to be an expert to use it.	
H You can download in seconds.	

(Total for Question 6 = 4 marks)

Booking a hotel

B 7 Listen to this telephone conversation.

Put a cross next to the correct answer.

> Numbers are common in listening exams. Don't lose marks by mixing them up.

Example: The caller wishes to book ...

A 1 room.	
B 2 rooms.	X
C 3 rooms.	

(i) On 14 May the hotel is ...

A closed.	
B full.	
C has only one room free.	

(ii) She finally decides to stay ...

A 3 nights.	
B 4 nights.	
C 5 nights.	

(iii) In the rooms she wants ...

A twin beds.	
B bunk beds.	
C double beds.	

(iv) The caller's name is señora...

A Lombarda.	
B Lambada.	
C La Bamba.	

(Total for Question 7 = 4 marks)

A new youth club

 8 Listen to an advert for a new youth club.

Which statements are true? Put a cross in the **four** correct boxes.

Example: It is not expensive.	X
A It is for all ages.	
B It is a safe place.	
C It is open every day.	
D It is a place to get advice.	
E You can meet lots of new people.	
F It is a brand new building.	
G There is a waiting list.	
H You can learn new skills.	

(Total for Question 8 = 4 marks)

Money matters

9 Listen to a banker who is giving advice. Answer the following questions **in English.**

(i) What does Mr Hernández say he is going to give advice about?

.... **(1 mark)**

(ii) What advice does he give if you are about to use an ATM? Give **two** facts.

....

.... **(2 marks)**

(iii) What does he say you should do if you suspect something is wrong with an ATM?

.... **(1 mark)**

(iv) What does he say you should do when actually using your card in the machine?

.... **(1 mark)**

(v) Why should you be as quick as possible?

.... **(1 mark)**

(vi) What tips does he give for once you have got money out of the ATM? Give two points.

....

.... **(2 marks)**

(Total for Question 9 = 8 marks)

The internet

10 Listen to some people discussing internet use at school. Complete the grids below. Write
your answers **in English.** Full sentences are not required.

Part A

POSITIVE ASPECTS	
(i)	
(ii)	
(iii)	
(iv)	

Part B

NEGATIVE ASPECTS	
(i)	
(ii)	
(iii)	
(iv)	

(Total for Question 10 = 4 marks)

Answers

Personal information

1 **(i)** Alejandro **(ii)** Fran
(iii) María **(iv)** Gloria

2 **(i)** B **(ii)** E **(iii)** F **(iv)** D

3 B, D, E, G

4 Part A: B, C, E, H
Part B: B, C, G, H

5 **(i)** 14 **(ii)** sporty
(iii) town **(iv)** grandparents

6 **(i)** E (whole family)
(ii) D (Grandmother)
(iii) B (father)
(iv) C (mother)

7 B, C, F, H

8 A, C, D, E

9 **(i)** Milagros **(ii)** Juan
(iii) Montse **(iv)** Jorge

10 A, B, C, G

11 **(i)** Isabel **(ii)** Hugo
(iii) Antonio **(iv)** Hugo

12 A, C, F, H

13 1 C 2 D 3 A 4 E

14 1 D 2 E 3 B 4 A

15 **(i)** C **(ii)** C **(iii)** B **(iv)** A

16 **(i)** E **(ii)** C **(iii)** B **(iv)** A

17 **(i)** Parents won't allow it. 20%
(ii) Feel ill. 1%
(iii) Don't feel like it. 7%
(iv) Have to look after younger brothers or sisters. 12%

18 ✓ C, D ✗ A, F

19 **(i)** Javier **(ii)** David
(iii) Luci **(iv)** David

20 **(i)** B **(ii)** D **(iii)** F **(iv)** A

21 B, D, E, G

22 **(i)** She spends most of her time watching films.
(ii) She hates documentaries.
(iii) She never watches soaps.
(iv) She says soaps are boring.

23 C, D, F, H

24 1 Funny / very friendly / not at all arrogant.
2 **(i)** Because he broke his leg during a football match.
(ii) He isn't American, and has a strong accent, so didn't expect that this would help him to be even more successful.

3 **(i)** Romantic, loyal and passionate heroes, also naughty and manipulative characters.
(ii) He has to spend a lot of time travelling. / He hates flying.

4 **(i)** He feels he doesn't belong anywhere, as he spends his life between the States and Málaga.

4 **(ii)** He misses his Spanish family.

25 **(i)** Daniela **(ii)** Hugo
(iii) Paco **(iv)** Beatriz

26 1 One of : He came here to study music / to improve his art (skills) / to get better opportunities.
2 **(a)** Breakfast is the best meal of the day. / He never used to eat it in Spain.
2 **(b)** He has lots of fans. / He is having some success.
3 **(a)** He plays and writes songs.
(b) He has a rest.
4 His ideas for songs won't let him.
5 He does a concert or radio appearance.
6 To promote his music.

27 **(a)** What can you do if you are young and you are bored?
(b) *Any two of:* It's the perfect solution. / It's fast. / It's easy. / You can do it from home.
(c) *Any two of:* You don't have to go out. / It's cheaper. / You can check the reviews (before choosing one).
(d) Even young people need to understand current affairs. / There are a lot of websites which offer up-to-date information.
(e) She's started learning French and taking guitar lessons.

28 **(i)** 6:15
(ii) Brush teeth, then get dressed.
(iii) On foot / walk.
(iv) Nothing / relax.

29 **(i)** early **(ii)** gets dressed
(iii) packs his bag **(iv)** has breakfast

30 **(i)** E **(ii)** D **(iii)** B **(iv)** C

31 B, D, E, H

32 Isabel = (iv) meat dishes
Gustavo = (i) tasty food
Sofía = not so healthy dishes (viii),
sweet dishes (viii)

33 **(i)** D **(ii)** C **(iii)** E **(iv)** F

34 A, C, F, G

35 **(i)** C **(ii)** B **(iii)** E **(iv)** F

36 B, D, E, G

37 (i) Claudia   (ii) Silvio
    (iii) Carmela   (iv) Claudia

38 (i) D   (ii) E   (iii) G   (iv) A

Out and about

1 (i) 100   (ii) Sunday
    (iii) 3 kilometres   (iv) smoke

2 B, C, G, H

3 B, C, F, H

4 (i) Sara C   (ii) Julio B
    (iii) Amina E   (iv) Serena F

5 (i) D   (ii) C   (iii) B   (iv) F

6 (i) B   (ii) F   (iii) A   (iv) D

7 (i) A   (ii) F   (iii) B   (iv) D

8 (i) D   (ii) C   (iii) E   (iv) F

9 (i) D   (ii) F   (iii) B   (iv) E

10 (i) A   (ii) D   (iii) B   (iv) F

11 (i) F   (ii) H   (iii) E   (iv) B

12 (i) D   (ii) A   (iii) E   (iv) F

13 (i) Consuelo   (ii) Santi
    (iii) Carmen   (iv) Consuelo

14 **Part A**
    (i) It is a residential area, in the south of Gran Canaria.
    (ii) There are very beautiful views.
    (iii) People are very friendly / welcoming.
    (iv) It can be very quiet. / There is not much to do for young people.

    Part B
    (i) To the sand dunes in Maspalomas. / To the pretty coves and beaches on the island.
    (ii) The restaurant is inside some real caves.
    (iii) Because he loves history.

15 (a) It was normal / uneventful.
    (b) Of impending doom / that something bad was going to happen.
    (c) The local mine collapsed (on 5/8/2010).
    (d) The men were trapped (for 69 days).
    (e) It is hard to find jobs there.
    (f) (i) Because her uncle escaped unharmed.
       (ii) Because he is not going to return to the mine.
    (g) He has got a job as a mechanic.

16 (i) B   (ii) D   (iii) A   (iv) F

17 (i) E   (ii) A   (iii) F   (iv) C

18 (a) Maruja   (b) Pablo
    (c) Pili   (d) Juli

19 (i) camp site   (ii) cousin's house
    (iii) youth hostel   (iv) hotel

20 (i) E   (ii) D   (iii) F   (iv) C

21 (i) D   (ii) F   (iii) G   (iv) E

22 C, F, G, H

23 B, C, E, G

24 B, D, E, G

25 Chus B, D   Gorka A, C

26 (i) E   (ii) D   (iii) A   (iv) C

27 (i) C   (ii) C   (iii) A   (iv) C

28 (a) Because they had a wonderful week the previous year.
    (b) 2 weeks.
    (c) Because they know that during the busy season, the camping books up quickly.
    (d) (i) Nearer the pool
       (ii) Because it is near all the other facilities. / It's easy to supervise the children.
    (e) If dogs are allowed and if there is an additional cost for them.

29 (i) B   (ii) D   (iii) A   (iv) C

30 (i) J   (ii) H   (iii) G   (iv) B

31 D, F, G, H

32 C, E, G, H

33 (i) A   (ii) C   (iii) E   (iv) D

34 (i) E   (ii) A   (iii) D   (iv) C

35 (i) A   (ii) B   (iii) C   (iv) A

36 (a) Kiko   (b) Tito
    (c) Sara   (d) Loli

37 **Advantages:**
    1 cheap way of travelling
    2 speed of travel (faster than coach)
    3 opportunity to meet people / make new friends
    4 safe / secure as lots of people do it

    Disadvantages:
    1 trains can be crowded
    2 noisy (couldn't sleep)
    3 difficult to get specific times and dates
    4 non-refundable tickets

Customer service and transactions

1 (i) ice cream   (ii) pleasant
    (iii) varied   (iv) expensive

2 (i) A   (ii) C   (iii) D   (iv) B

3 (i) C   (ii) E   (iii) B   (iv) D

4 (i) C   (ii) F   (iii) D   (iv) E

5 (i) A   (ii) F   (iii) B   (iv) D

6 (i) A   (ii) C   (iii) A   (iv) C

7 (i) F   (ii) D   (iii) C   (iv) A

8 **(i)** Raquel   **(ii)** Iago
   (iii) Mimi   **(iv)** Iago

9 B, C, E, G

10 **(i)** C Marta   **(ii)** B Nadia
    (iii) A Alejandro **(iv)** B Nadia

11 **(a)** Any two of: increase of online shopping / low earnings / cost of rent / cost of parking
    (b) Any two of: cheaper / more convenient / can do this from home
    (c) Any two of: survey local residents / park and ride schemes / tackle crime
    (d) Contact the help desk.
    (e) Town centres will disappear forever.

12 C, E, F, H

13 A, B, D, G

14 **(i)** E   **(ii)** A   **(iii)** D   **(iv)** F

15 **(i)** E   **(ii)** C   **(iii)** B   **(iv)** D

16 A, B, D, H

17 **(a)** About opening hours during holidays.
    (b) From 8 am to 2 pm.
    (c) On 27th December.
    (d) Big sales start.

18 **(a)** Paco   **(b)** Juan
    (c) Marina   **(d)** Patri

19 **(i)** E   **(ii)** C   **(iii)** B   **(iv)** A

20 Positive: (i), (ii)
    Negative: (iii), (iv)

21 B, D, F, H

22 **(i)** Paquito   **(ii)** David
    (iii) Daniela **(iv)** Julieta

23 **(i)** A   **(ii)** B   **(iii)** D   **(iv)** I

24 **(i)** B   **(ii)** C   **(iii)** A   **(iv)** E

25 **(i)** Vicente E   **(ii)** Olivia B
    (iii) Simón C   **(iv)** Begoña F

26 **(i)** Antonia   **(ii)** Elvira
    (iii) Pepito   **(iv)** Elvira

27 **(i)** Ana   **(ii)** Ana
    (iii) Inés   **(iv)** Pablo

28

Problem	Solution
(i) Trains are more prone to delays than other modes of transport.	**(i)** Leave plenty of time or go by another means.
(ii) Difficult to buy tickets at station during rush hour / long queues might make you miss your train.	**(ii)** Buy tickets in advance, preferably online or by phone.
(iii) Actually getting to the station can be difficult, sometimes involving other means of transport.	**(iii)** Buy a bicycle. It costs little and you can take it on the train.
(iv) Carrying luggage about can be inconvenient.	**(iv)** Plan ahead. Call a taxi or get a friend to take you to the station.

29 **(a)** Wednesday.
    (b) Not direct. / Have to change trains in Tarragona.
    (c) Two.
    (d) 72.

30 B, C, E, G

31 Likes: C, G   Dislikes: B, D

32 **Part A**
    (i) *Any one of:* She was mugged (robbed). / She fell to the ground. / She had to be taken to hospital.
    (ii) *Any one of:* She is okay. / She is very frightened. / She is a little afraid to go out.
    (iii) She had 100 euros cash on her, which was stolen.
    (iv) To open a bank account.
    Part B
    Advantages:
    (i) It will keep your money safe.
    (ii) Banks often give you freebies, e.g. mobile phones, special discounts.
    Disadvantages:
    (i) You need to show your ID.
    (ii) You might get into debt

33
- **(i)** He has lost his suitcase.
- **(ii)** On the plane.
- **(iii)** On Wednesday.
- **(iv)** He has to buy clothes.
- **(v)** He wants her to ask mum to contact the airport.

34
- **(a)** Yesterday morning.
- **(b)** Her handbag.
- **(c)** *Any two of:* She was waiting at bus stop. / Her phone rang. / She put bag down to answer. / A man snatched the bag.
- **(d)** *Any two of:* He was quite young / pale / very thin / wearing sunglasses.
- **(e)** **(i)** It is a black leather bag, a designer label. She had her purse with fifty euros and keys inside.
  - **(ii)** She is asked to complete a form / contact her insurance company.

35 **(i)** G **(ii)** F **(iii)** H **(iv)** A

36
- **(a)** Lupe **(b)** Begoña
- **(c)** Urbano **(d)** Fabio

Future plans, education and work

1 **(i)** B **(ii)** C **(iii)** F **(iv)** D
2 **(i)** B **(ii)** A **(iii)** F **(iv)** D
3 B, D, F, H
4 **(i)** A **(ii)** B **(iii)** B **(iv)** A
5 **(i)** A **(ii)** C **(iii)** F **(iv)** B
6 **(i)** B **(ii)** C **(iii)** A **(iv)** B
7 B, C, E, H
8 ☺ **(i)** D **(ii)** A
☹ **(i)** G **(ii)** C
9 **(i)** Ricardo **(ii)** Marina
(iii) Julia **(iv)** Ana
10 **(i)** G **(ii)** F **(iii)** B **(iv)** D
11 **(i)** Future **(ii)** Present
(iii) Present **(iv)** Past
12 **(a)** Íker **(b)** Sergio
(c) Cristina **(d)** Carolina
13 **(i)** Alberto **(ii)** Maxi & Alberto
(iii) Marta
14 **(i)** E **(ii)** F **(iii)** A **(iv)** B
15 **(i)** C **(ii)** D **(iii)** G **(iv)** A
16 **(a)** María **(b)** Íñigo
(c) Jesús **(d)** Borja
17 **(i)** Dolores **(ii)** Federico
(iii) Ángela **(iv)** Martín
18 **(i)** C **(ii)** C **(iii)** C **(iv)** B
19 **(i)** Felipe B **(ii)** Susana D
(iii) Daniel C **(v)** Kiko E

20
- **(i)** (next) March
- **(ii)** lots of different jobs
- **(iii)** *Any two of:* people with or without training/education / people willing to learn / people who get on well with others
- **(iv)** flexible hours / good salary
- **(v)** go to hotel web page for more information and an application form / visit hotel open day (6th February)

21 **(i)** D **(ii)** B **(iii)** F **(iv)** E

22
- **(i)** There are lots of people chasing one job.
- **(ii)** *Any two of:* printed (not hand-written) / factual / positive / include achievements and successes.
- **(iii)** Correct spelling and grammar.
- **(iv)** It is no good – the CV has to be specific to the job being applied for.
- **(v)** Research to find out about the company you are sending your CV to.
- **(vi)** You can include information that would attract prospective employers.

23 **(i)** C **(ii)** B **(iii)** B **(iv)** A

24
- **(i)** walk confidently / shake hands firmly – gives a good impression
- **(ii)** don't sit down without being asked to / smile – is polite
- **(iii)** keep eye contact – shows your interest
- **(iv)** tell the truth – lies are obvious

25 **(a)** 16 **(b)** English
(c) hard-working **(d)** August
26 B, C, E, H
27 A (activity leader) + C E F
28 **(i)** clothes **(ii)** hours
(iii) fun **(iv)** good
29 **(i)** D **(ii)** E **(iii)** B **(iv)** A
30 **(i)** Alicia **(ii)** Catalina
(iii) Manu **(iv)** Fernando
31 B, D, E, H
32 **(i)** ☹ **(ii)** ☹ **(iii)** ☹ **(iv)** ☺
33 A, C, E, H
34 **Part A**
(i) A **(ii)** C **(iii)** C **(iv)** take part
Part B
B, D, F, G
35 **(a)** Every afternoon/evening.
(b) About four hours.
(c) English.
(d) Because he thinks it's too complicated.

36 Ana – texting + downloading music
Daniel – looking for work + sharing photos

37 (a) to advise students about internet safety

(b) examine / review their blogs

(c) included her personal details

(d) copied the school crest

(e) *Any two of:* trace the town from the school crest / find the park she goes to every day to meet friends / recognise her from the photo that shows her age clearly

(f) *Any two of:* more careful now / reviewed and changed web content / gives out less info when chatting online

Grammar

Nouns and articles

1 1 la   2 el   3 las   4 los
  5 la   6 el   7 las   8 los
  9 el   10 la

2 1 las   2 un   3 el   4 los
  5 una   6 un   7 el   8 El

3 2 Mi padre es ~~un~~ dentista y mi madre es ~~una~~ enfermera.

3 Hablo ~~el~~ español y ~~el~~ sueco.

4 Escribo con ~~un~~ lápiz en mi clase de matemáticas.

5 El sábado voy a ~~la~~ casa de mis abuelos.

6 Se pueden reservar dos habitaciones con ~~una~~ ducha.

2 Adjectives

1 1 adosada   2 traviesos
  3 rojo   4 interesantes
  5 español   6 simpáticas
  7 preciosa   8 baratos

2 1 lujoso   2 cómodos
  3 bueno   4 impresionante
  5 limpia   6 útiles

3 1 En Inglaterra hay **poca** gente que habla muy bien griego.

2 Lo mejor es que tiene un jardín **bonito**.

3 Estamos **contentas** porque hace buen tiempo.

4 En el futuro habrá una **gran** estatua aquí en la plaza.

5 Nuestro apartamento está en el **primer** piso.

6 Mis primas son **alemanas** pero viven en Escocia.

Possessives and pronouns

1

English	Spanish singular	Spanish plural
my	mi	**mis**
your	**tu**	tus
his / her / its	**su**	**sus**
our	**nuestro / nuestra**	nuestros / nuestras
your	**vuestro / vuestra**	**vuestros / vuestras**
their	su	**sus**

2 1 Mi   2 Su   3 Sus
  4 Mis   5 Su

3 1 el mío   2 las suyas
  3 el nuestro   4 el tuyo

4 1 María tiene un gato que es negro y pequeño.

2 Vivimos en un pueblo que está en el norte de Inglaterra.

3 En la clase de literatura tengo que leer un libro que es muy aburrido.

Comparisons

1 1 Mi madre es **más delgada que** mi padre.

2 Mariela es **menos paciente que** Francisco.

3 Este autobús es **más lento que** el tren.

4 La fruta es **tan sana / saludable como** las verduras.

5 Esta camisa es **tan cara como** aquella chaqueta.

2 1 el mejor

2 los peores

3 la más pequeña

4 los más inteligentes

5 las menos aburridas

3 1 Mi coche es el más barato.

2 Mi primo/a es más perezoso/a que tu tío.

3 Su móvil es pequeñísimo.

4 El examen de español es facilísimo.

5 Las películas de terror son tan emocionantes como las películas de acción.

6 ¡Mi instituto es el más feo!

7 Las ciencias son menos aburridas que la geografía.

8 Messi es el mejor.

Other adjectives

1

Masc sing	Fem sing	Masc plural	Fem plural	Meaning
este	**esta**	**estos**	estas	this / these
ese	esa	**esos**	esas	that / those
aquel	**aquella**	aquellos	**aquellas**	that (over there) / those (over there)

2
1 estas botas 2 esta camiseta
3 aquella chica 4 esos plátanos
5 ese móvil 6 aquellas revistas
7 este iPod 8 esa película
9 aquel tren 10 estos sombreros
11 esas fresas 12 aquellos chicos

3
1 cada 2 misma
3 algunas 4 todos 5 mismo

4
1 Todos 2 Algunos 3 Todos
4 algunos 5 misma 6 mismos

Pronouns

1

yo	**I**
tú	you
él	he
ella	**she**
nosotros	we (masc.)
nosotras	**we (fem.)**
vosotros	**you (masc.)**
vosotras	you (fem.)
ellos	**they (masc.)**
ellas	they (fem.)

2
1 Las hemos perdido.
2 La han perdido.
3 Teresa lo come.
4 Lo compro.
5 No la bebo.
6 No la lavo.
7 Lo quiero escribir. / Quiero escribirlo.
8 No quiero leerla. / No la quiero leer.
9 La necesito ahora.
10 Vamos a venderla. / La vamos a vender.

3
1 I am going to call him/her this afternoon.
2 I visited them yesterday.
3 I will do it if I have time.
4 I sell them at the market.
5 Have you seen them?
6 Vino a visitarme a casa. / Me vino a visitar a casa.
7 Me mandaron la reserva.
8 Los / Las voy a comprar por Internet. / Voy a comprarlos/comprarlas por Internet.

The present tense

1
1 vivimos 2 bailan 3 vendo
4 lleváis 5 odias 6 come
7 salimos 8 escucha

2
1 comen 2 vivimos 3 tienes
4 hablan 5 debe 6 grita
7 chateo 8 lee 9 piensa
10 Podéis

3
1 cenamos 2 trabajan
3 desayuno 4 pone
5 compramos 6 cuestan
7 Quiero 8 piden

Reflexives and irregulars

1

me	afeito
te	afeitas
se	afeita
nos	afeitamos
os	afeitáis
se	afeitan
me	visto
te	vistes
se	viste
nos	vestimos
os	vestís
se	visten

2 **1** se   **2** se   **3** te
   4 se   **5** se   **6** Nos
   7 Os   **8** Te

3 Todos los días Olivia **se levanta** temprano para ir a trabajar. **Trabaja** en una tienda de ropa famosa. Primero **se lava** los dientes y luego **se ducha** y **se viste**. **Baja** las escaleras y **desayuna** cereales con fruta. Siempre **se peina** en la cocina. Después, **se lava** la cara en el cuarto de baño que está abajo, al lado de la cocina. **Se pone** la chaqueta y **sale** a las ocho y media porque el autobús llega a las nueve menos cuarto. **Vuelve** a casa a las siete de la tarde.

Ser and estar

1 **1** está   **2** son   **3** Soy   **4** es
   5 Son   **6** está   **7** Estáis
   8 Estamos

2 **1** Where is the bank? ("estar" for location)
   2 My grandmothers are very generous. ("ser" for characteristics)
   3 I am from Madrid but I work in Barcelona. ("ser" for where you are from)
   4 The dress is green with white flowers. ("ser" for colours)
   5 It's four thirty in the afternoon. ("ser" for time)
   6 The wardrobe is opposite the door. ("estar" for location)
   7 You are (all) very sad today because the holidays have finished. ("estar" for moods)
   8 We are ready for the drama exam. ("estar" for meaning "ready" not "clever")

3 1, 4, 5, 7 – ✓
   2 Mi amigo **es** inteligente y tiene el pelo negro.
   3 Me duele la cabeza y **estoy** enfermo.
   6 Mi madre **es** dependienta y mi padre **es** ingeniero.
   8 Mi casa **es** bastante pequeña – tiene solo un dormitorio.

The gerund

1 **1** comiendo – eating
   2 saltando – jumping
   3 **corriendo – runnning**
   4 **tomando – taking (drinking/eating)**
   5 **durmiendo – sleeping**
   6 **asistiendo – attending**
   7 **escribiendo - writing**
   8 **escuchando – listening**
   9 **aprendiendo – learning**
   10 **pudiendo – being able to**

2 **1** Está montando en bicicleta.
   2 Estoy escuchando música.
   3 Están navegando por Internet.
   4 Estamos viendo una película.
   5 Estás hablando con amigos.

3 **1** Estaba haciendo vela cuando llegó la tormenta.
   2 Estaban comiendo cuando su madre les llamó.
   3 Estábamos tomando el sol cuando empezó a llover.
   4 Estabas cantando cuando salió el tren.
   5 Estábamos viendo la tele cuando nuestro padre volvió a casa.
   6 Estaba jugando a los videojuegos cuando llamó.
   7 Estabais escuchando al profesor cuando entró el perro.
   8 Estaba nadando en el mar cuando el tiburón apareció.

The preterite tense

1 **1** sacaron   **2** volvimos   **3** compró
   4 llegaste   **5** trabajasteis   **6** fue
   7 di   **8** tuvimos   **9** visitaron
   10 bebió

2 **1** fui   **2** tuvimos   **3** dieron
   4 fue   **5** me levanté, me vestí
   6 hicieron   **7** dijo   **8** fue
   9 Hice   **10** tuve

3 **Fui** al cine con mis amigos y **vimos** una película de acción. Después **comimos** en un restaurante italiano. **Comí** una pizza con jamón y queso, y mi amiga Lola **comió** pollo con pasta. **Bebimos** zumo de manzana y mi amigo Tom **comió** una torta de chocolate pero yo no **comí** postre. Después del restaurante **fui** en tren a casa de mi prima. El viaje **fue** largo y aburrido. **Volví** a casa y me **acosté** a las once de la noche.

The imperfect tense

2 De pequeños <u>nadábamos</u> en el mar todas las semanas. ✓

3 <u>Había</u> mucha gente en el museo y las estatuas <u>eran</u> preciosas. ✓

5 Cuando <u>eran</u> más jóvenes, no <u>comían</u> tomate ni lechuga.

8 Me <u>ponía</u> nervioso cada vez que <u>hacía</u> una prueba de vocabulario. ✓

10 <u>Nevaba</u> todos los días y <u>hacía</u> un frío horrible. ✓

2 1 Last Wednesday we went to the swimming pool and we swam for an hour and a half. (preterite for a completed action in the past)

2 When we were kids, we used to swim in the sea every week. (imperfect for "used to")

3 There were lots of people in the museum and the statues were beautiful. (imperfect for descriptions)

4 My father prepared a vegetarian supper for us. (preterite for a completed action in the past)

5 When they were younger, they didn't eat tomatoes or lettuce. (imperfect to describe repeated actions in the past)

6 Gabriela arrived in Madrid by train to start her new job. (preterite for a completed action in the past)

7 Yesterday we met in the café and we talked all afternoon. (preterite for a completed action in the past)

8 I used to get nervous every time I did a vocabulary test. (imperfect for "used to")

9 I had a great time because it was sunny and it didn't rain. (preterite for a completed action in the past)

10 It snowed every day and it was terribly cold. (imperfect for descriptions)

3 1 tenía   2 vivía   3 Estaba
4 pasé   5 trabajaban   6 gastó
7 comíamos   8 jugué

The future tense

1 1 jugar   2 Va   3 a   4 voy
5 Vas   6 Vais   7 va   8 ir
9 vamos   10 Voy

2 1 Vamos a ver la película.
2 No trabajaré los lunes.
3 Van a coger el metro.
4 Irá a Inglaterra.
5 Van a jugar con mi hermano.
6 Irás a España.

3 1 va a ir   2 voy a ir
3 voy a tomar   4 voy a tener
5 Voy a trabajar   6 Va a ser
7 va a ser   8 va a seguir
9 va a vivir

The conditional

1 1 compraríamos – we would buy
2 saldrían – they would go out
3 trabajaríais – you (all) would work
4 estaría – he / she / it would be
5 jugarías – you would play
6 vendríamos – we would come
7 podrías – you could
8 habría – there would be

2 1 iría   2 tomarían
3 trabajaría   4 ganaríamos
5 habría   6 usaría
7 malgastarían   8 lucharían
9 ganaría   10 compartiríamos

3 NB All answers can use either *podrías* or *deberías*. Some answers are interchangeable.
1 Podrías evitar el estrés.
2 Podrías comer más fruta y verduras.
3 Deberías hacer más ejercicio.
4 Deberías ir al médico.
5 Deberías acostarte temprano.
6 Podrías ir al dentista.
7 Deberías consumir menos energía.
8 Podrías comprar ropa de segunda mano.

Thr perfect and pluperfect tenses

1

	Perfect tense	Pluperfect tense	+ past participles
yo	he	**había**	hablado comido vivido
tú	**has**	**habías**	
él / ella / usted	**ha**	había	
nosotros / nosotras	hemos	**habíamos**	
vosotros / vosotras	**habéis**	**habíais**	
ellos / ellas / ustedes	**han**	habían	

2 1   We have lost our car.
    2   Have you studied Spanish?
    3   They have bought a laptop.
    4   I have done my homework
    5   We have seen a very informative documentary.
    6   Me he roto el brazo.
    7   Han perdido la maleta.
    8   Hemos comido muchos caramelos.
    9   ¿Has visitado el museo hoy?
    10   El dependiente / La dependienta ha abierto la tienda.

3 2 había perdido   3 había nadado
    4 había hecho   5 había dejado
    6 había encontrado

Giving instructions

1 1   Dobla a la derecha.
    2   Cruza la plaza.
    3   Pasa el puente.
    4   Ten cuidado.
    5   Ven aquí.
    6   Canta más bajo.
    7   Lee en voz alta.
    8   Escucha bien.
    9   Pon la mesa.
    10   Haz este ejercicio.

2 1   Doblad a la derecha.
    2   Cruzad la plaza.
    3   Pasad el puente.
    4   Tened cuidado.
    5   Venid aquí.
    6   Cantad más bajo.
    7   Leed en voz alta.
    8   Escuchad bien.
    9   Poned la mesa.
    10   Haced este ejercicio.

3 1   ¡Descarga la música!
    2   ¡Doblad a la izquierda!
    3   ¡Quita la mesa!
    4   ¡Haz la cama!
    5   ¡Pasad la aspiradora!

The present subjunctive

1 1   hable   2   coman   3   vaya
    4   **vivas**   5   **trabajéis**   6   **salga**
    7   **pueda**   8   **hagan**   9   **encuentre**
    10   **seamos**

2 1   No comas este pastel.
    2   No compres aquel vestido.
    3   No tomes estas pastillas.
    4   No bebas un vaso de zumo de naranja.
    5   No veas esta película romántica.
    6   No firmes aquí.
    7   No rellenes el formulario.
    8   No saltes tres veces.

3 1   trabajen   2   haga   3   tengamos
    4   sean   5   vaya   6   compren

Negatives

1 1   No estudio geografía.
    2   No vamos a las afueras.
    3   Ricardo no compró una moto nueva.
    4   Sus padres no vieron la tele.
    5   No voy a ir a Francia la semana que viene.

2 1   e   2   d   3   b   4   g
    5   a/f   6   a/f   7   c

3 1   Mis profesores no enseñan nunca cómo teclear.
    2   En mi casa no tuvimos jamás una sala de juegos.
    3   No me he quemado nunca los brazos.
    4   Aquí no tengo ni vestidos, ni faldas, ni camisetas.
    5   No vas a comprar ningún coche.
    6   Mis padres no escuchan a nadie.

4 **1** Por la tarde nunca bebemos / tomamos café. / Por la tarde no bebemos / tomamos nunca café.

2 No plancho, ni cocino, ni limpio.

3 No hablan ningún idioma.

4 No podemos hablar con nadie durante el examen.

5 No fumaré jamás / nunca porque es una pérdida de tiempo. / Jamás / Nunca fumaré porque es una pérdida de tiempo.

Special verbs

1

me	gusta (sing) gustan (plural)	I like
te		you like
le		he / she / it likes
nos		we like
os		you (all) like
les		they like

2 1, 3 – ✓

2 Nos **apetece** ir al teatro mañana.

4 No nos **gusta** la contaminación atmosférica.

5 ¿Te **hacen** falta unas toallas?

3 **1** Nos hace falta un abrigo.

2 Os encantan los caballos negros.

3 A María le gustan aquellos zapatos.

4 Te quedan veinte euros para comprar el regalo.

5 Me duele la garganta todo el tiempo.

6 Les encantan los rascacielos porque son modernos.

Por and *para*

1 **1** For my birthday I want a new mobile phone.

2 My friend works for a lawyer.

3 Apps for the iPhone are incredible.

4 I eat a lot of vegetables and fish in order to keep fit.

5 You need the key to get into the house.

6 Smoking is very bad for your health.

7 They are going to organise a party to celebrate the end of the course.

8 For me, sports are always fun.

2 **1** El coche rojo pasó por las calles antiguas.

2 Normalmente por la mañana me gusta desayunar cereales y fruta.

3 Mandé la reserva por correo electrónico.

4 Me gustaría cambiar este jersey por otro.

5 En la tienda ganamos diez euros por hora.

6 Había mucha basura por todas partes.

3 **1** Para **2** para **3** por
4 para **5** para

Questions and exclamations

1 Why? – **¿Por qué?**

What? – **¿Qué?**

When? – **¿Cuándo?**

How? – **¿Cómo?**

Where? – **¿Dónde?**

Where to? – **¿Adónde?**

Which? – **¿Cuál?**

Which ones? – **¿Cuáles?**

How much? – **¿Cuánto?**

How many? – **¿Cuántos?**

2

1	F
2	E
3	G
4	J
5	A
6	C
7	I
8	B
9	H
10	D

3 **1** horror **2** Cuánto **3** Dónde
4 guay **5** rollo

Connectives and adverbs

1 **1** rápidamente **2** difícilmente
3 lentamente **4** alegremente
5 tranquilamente

2

1	L
2	E
3	A
4	K
5	D
6	B
7	G
8	J
9	F
10	I
11	C
12	H

3
1. Sus padres cantan mal en la iglesia.
2. No hablo mucho porque soy tímido.
3. El tren pasa rápidamente por el túnel.
4. Los pendientes son demasiado caros.
5. A menudo comemos huevos por la mañana. / Comemos a menudo huevos por la mañana.
6. si / porque
7. porque
8. pero

Numbers

1
A veinte 20
B cuarenta y ocho 48
C nueve 9
D cien 100
E catorce 14
F mil 1000
G trescientos 300
H cincuenta y siete 57
I veintitrés 23
J quince 15
K diecinueve 19
L quinientos 500
M un millón 1000000
N novecientos 900
O ochenta y ocho 88
P setenta y seis 76
Q sesenta y siete 67
R diez 10
S cero 0
T veintinueve 29

2
1. mil novecientos noventa y nueve
2. el diez de octubre
3. el primero/uno de enero
4. el tres de marzo
5. dos mil trece
6. el dieciséis de noviembre
7. el treinta de mayo
8. mil novecientos sesenta y ocho
9. dos mil dos
10. el veintiuno de abril

3
1. 20, 25 € veinte euros con veinticinco
2. 59, 10 € cincuenta y nueve euros con diez
3. 100,75 € cien euros con setenta y cinco
4. 87 € ochenta y siete euros
5. 45,20 € cuarenta y cinco euros con veinte
6. 7,99 € siete euros con noventa y nueve
7. 86,70 € ochenta y seis euros con setenta
8. 30,65 € treinta euros con sesenta y cinco

Practice Exam

Reading

1 (i) A (ii) C (iii) D (iv) E

2 (i) Elvira B (ii) Fátima D
(iii) Juan C (iv) Nando E

3 (i) Mar D (ii) Ángel E
(iii) Isabel B (iv) Martín C

4 B, E, F, G

5 B, C, D, G

6 B, E, F, G

7 B, D, F, H

8 (i) B (ii) C (iii) B (iv) C

9

Problem	Person	Advice (any of...)
parents	E	Sit down and talk things over calmly / reach an agreement.
no money	B	Find things to do with your friends which don't cost very much / be imaginative.
worried about the future	D	Work hard at school / do a lot of activities outside school to have an interesting CV.
being lonely	C	Join a local club / take up a new sport or hobby.

Listening

1   1 B   2 A   3 F   4 D

2   **(i)** C   **(ii)** E   **(iii)** F   **(iv)** D

3   **(i)** B   **(ii)** H   **(iii)** C   **(iv)** D

4   **1** Conchi   **2** Ana
    3 David   **4** Conchi

5   **(i)**   Flor A   **(ii)**   Federico F
    (iii) Clara E   **(iv)**   Seve D

6   C, D, F, H

7   **(i)** B   **(ii)** C   **(iii)** C   **(iv)** A

8   B, D, E, H

9   **(i)**   Safety
    (ii)   *Any two of:* look around for people
              nearby / look to see if the machine
              looks odd or has been tampered with
              / if you suspect something is wrong
              don't use it
    (iii) *Any one of:* don't use it / go to
              another ATM / tell the bank
    (iv) When typing in your number, cover
              it with your hand.
    (v)   *Any one of:* so no-one can see your
              number / to avoid getting mugged
    (vi) *Any two of:* put your cash away
              immediately / put your receipt away
              immediately / don't hang around
              (waste time) at the maching / walk
              away quickly / count your money in
              a safe place.

10 **Positive**
    Any four of: social networking (contact
    with friends and family) / research,
    information (for homework) /
    entertainment (games) / help and advice
    /
    catch up TV and films
    Negative
    Any four from: time wasting / cost /
    dangers for children and teenagers /
    fraud / viruses

Published by Pearson Education Limited, Edinburgh Gate, Harlow, Essex, CM20 2JE.

www.pearsonschoolsandfecolleges.co.uk

Copies of official specifications for all Edexcel qualifications may be found on the Edexcel website: www. edexcel.com

Text © Pearson Education Limited 2013
Audio © Pearson Education Limited / Tom Dick and Debbie Productions
MFL Series Editor Julie Green
Edited by Ruth Manteca, Tracy Traynor and Sue Chapple
Typeset by Kamae Design, Oxford
Original illustrations © Pearson Education Limited 2013
Illustrations by KJA Artists
Cover illustration by Miriam Sturdee

First published 2013

16 15 14
10 9 8 7 6 5 4

British Library Cataloguing in Publication Data
A catalogue record for this book is available from the British Library

ISBN 978 1 446 90351 3

Printed in Slovakia by Neografia

In the writing of this book, no Edexcel examiners authored sections relevant to examination papers for which they have responsibility.